SAINT MAXIMUS THE CONFESSOR

On the Ecclesiastical Mystagogy

T0335149

ST VLADIMIR'S SEMINARY PRESS
Popular Patristics Series
Number 59

The Popular Patristics Series published by St Vladimir's Seminary Press provides readable and accurate translations of a wide range of early Christian literature to a wide audience—students of Christian history to lay Christians reading for spiritual benefit. Recognized scholars in their fields provide short but comprehensive and clear introductions to the material. The texts include classics of Christian literature, thematic volumes, collections of homilies, letters on spiritual counsel, and poetical works from a variety of geographical contexts and historical backgrounds. The mission of the series is to mine the riches of the early Church and to make these treasures available to all.

Series Editor
BOGDAN BUCUR

Associate Editor
IGNATIUS GREEN

* * *

Series Editor
1999–2020
JOHN BEHR

SAINT MAXIMUS THE CONFESSOR

On the Ecclesiastical Mystagogy

Introduction, Translation, Notes, and Bibliography by

JONATHAN J. ARMSTRONG

In Collaboration with

SHAWN FOWLER and TIM WELLINGS

ST VLADIMIR'S SEMINARY PRESS

YONKERS, NEW YORK

2019

Library of Congress Control Number: 2019943984

ISBN 978–088141–647–3 (paper)
ISBN 978–088141–652–7 (electronic)
ISSN 1555–5755

PRINTED IN THE UNITED STATES OF AMERICA

To Sophie
ὁ λόγος τοῦ Χριστοῦ ἐνοικείτω ἐν ὑμῖν
πλουσίως ἐν πάσῃ σοφίᾳ

Contents

Preface

In 2013, while completing revisions for the translation of Eusebius of Caesarea's *Commentary on Isaiah* (IVP Academic), I started to search for a new translation project of one of the Church fathers. I had recently founded the Ancient Christian Studies Honors Program at Moody Bible Institute—Spokane, and I planned to invite students from my advanced Greek seminar to join me in the translation process. That year at the North American Patristics Society meeting in Chicago, Bart Janssens of Brepols recommended to me *The Mystagogy of the Church* by Maximus the Confessor because the critical edition of the Greek text had been published in 2011 in the *Corpus Christianorum Series Greca*. Julian Stead published a first English translation of the text in 1982,[1] followed by George C. Berthold's more literal and philosophically attuned translation in the *Classics of Western Spirituality* series in 1985.[2] Previous English translations had not been based on a critical edition of the Greek text, and therefore an opportunity presented itself to produce a new translation of this key text concerning the ancient Byzantine theology of the liturgy.

In the fall semester of 2013, Shawn Fowler, Tim Wellings, and I set to work. For many hours each week during the first three semesters of the project, we sat around a table with our copies of the Greek text and computers spread out in front of us, reaching for the pile of dictionaries at the center of the table in rotation. I soon discovered that, because we were working as a committee, we were able

[1] Julian Stead, O.S.B., *The Church, the Liturgy and the Soul of Man: The* Mystagogia *of Maximus the Confessor* (Still River, MA: St. Bede's Publications, 1982).

[2] George C. Berthold, *Maximus Confessor: Selected Writings* (New York: Paulist Press, 1985).

together to tease out many more of the philosophical nuances and to develop a far more consistent translation than I would have been able to do had I worked alone. Poring over each line, we weighed our provisional translations against Stead's and Berthold's and examined Maximus' use of terms across the treatise, all the while scouring the standard lexicons for any shade of meaning that might set the passage in a different light. The process was painstaking but the result was enormously rewarding. Shawn Fowler and Tim Wellings completed a third and final semester with the project in the fall of 2014, and Kevin Illidge, Kyle Rouse, and Kindra Thurman joined the translation seminar for the academic year of 2014–2015. Michael Kirchdorfer, Randy Garcia, Derek Beehler, and I continued to revise and correct our draft translation during the academic year of 2015–2016. During the three years that my advanced Greek students and I labored over the translation, we worked through the Greek text three times. I then worked through the entire text again for a fourth time during the summer of 2016 in order to produce the final version. In retrospect, I can affirm that the density and intricacy of Maximus' Greek demands reading again and again; the approach to the project as a translation seminar proved to be felicitous.

I am especially pleased to see the publication of this translation as it represents the fruit of so many rich friendships and countless conversations. Maximus the Confessor became something of a permanent fixture in our Ancient Christian Studies Honors Program, not simply because a number of us were involved in the translation project but because the exercise of reading Maximus was renewing our theology and reorienting our conversations with our fellow students and tutors in the honors program. We were predominantly evangelical, but we discovered the mystical theology of Maximus the Confessor to be a key that opened doors of understanding for us into the world of ecumenical relationships, whether it be with the Eastern Orthodox communion or the Roman Catholic, Anglican, or Pentecostal world.

Finally, I want to thank the St Vladimir's Seminary Press team: Fr John Behr, the Popular Patristics Series editor who agreed to take this project and provided helpful suggestions for the introduction, to Fr Ignatius Green, who edited the text and guided the work through the production process, and Fr Benedict Churchill, who prepared the Greek text that appears in this edition (this is a "working" edition that uses the Migne as a base text, with some modifications in capitalization and punctuation, which notes or incorporates significant variants from the critical edition, without noting minor differences, e.g., orthographical variants and transpositions that do not change the text's meaning; PG 91 column locations are given in-line in the Greek text, and page and line numbers referring to the critical edition are placed in the margin next to the English translation).

Jonathan J. Armstrong, Ph.D.

Introduction

By Jonathan J. Armstrong, Ph.D.

Maximus the Confessor (*c.* 580–662) is considered the leading theologian of the seventh century and among the most influential of the early Church fathers. In his five-volume series, *The Christian Tradition: A History of the Development of Doctrine*, Jaroslav Pelikan opens his work on Eastern Christianity with this statement on Maximus the Confessor: "The dominant figure in the development of Christian doctrine in the East during the seventh century was Maximus the Confessor, whom modern historians have acclaimed as 'the most universal spirit of the seventh century and perhaps the last independent thinker among the theologians of the Byzantine Church,' as 'probably the only productive thinker of the entire century,' and as 'the real father of Byzantine theology.' "[1] Adroit diplomat, introspective ascetic, dogmatic theologian, resolute confessor who came to stand between pope in Rome and the Byzantine emperor, Maximus' biography is as enigmatic and mysterious as his theology. He lived in both Constantinople at the center of the Byzantine world and in Carthage in Roman North Africa; he wrote his treatises in the Greek language but collaborated with the Latin Church in order to secure the condemnation of Monothelitism, which had been favored by the Byzantine Emperor. When on trial before the senate in Constantinople and asked why he loved the Romans but hated the Greeks, Maximus responded: "We have a precept which says not to hate anyone. I love the Romans as those who share the same faith,

---

[1] *The Spirit of Eastern Christendom (600–1700)*, in *The Christian Tradition*, vol. 2 (Chicago: University of Chicago Press, 1974), 8.

and the Greeks as sharing the same language."[2] Maximus proved to be a genius in theological synthesis, weaving together the principal strands of the tradition before him into an almost perfectly unified system. Hans Urs von Balthasar, the twentieth-century Jesuit theologian, could write of Maximus: "He was a contemplative biblical theologian, a philosopher of Aristotelian training, a mystic in the great Neoplatonic tradition of Gregory of Nyssa and Pseudo-Dionysius the Areopagite, an enthusiastic theologian of the Word along the lines of Origen, a strict monk of the Evagrian tradition, and—finally and before all else—a man of the Church, who fought and who gave his life in witness for the orthodox Christology of Chalcedon and for a Church centered in Rome."[3] While contemporary readers may tend to conceptualize Maximus as a representative of early eastern Christianity, Andrew Louth rightly notes the complexity of categorizing Maximus' theology when he writes: "It seems to me that to talk of East and West in the context of the seventh century is to allow oneself too few points of the compass."[4]

I. The Life of Maximus the Confessor:

There are several sources of information concerning Maximus' life. First, we find biographical comments in Maximus' own literary corpus. Second, the *Vita Maximi*, written in Greek in the tenth-century, is our primary source of information concerning the life of Maximus.[5] The *Vita Maximi* also exists in a Georgian version, and the Georgian version includes some information that supplements the Greek tradition. Third, there is also a Syriac *Life of Maximus*,

[2] "The Trial of Maximus: An Account of the Proceedings Which Took Place between the Lord Abbot Maximus and His Companions and the Officials in the Chamber," in *Maximus Confessor: Selected Writings*, trans., George C. Berthold (New York: Paulist Press, 1985), 26.

[3] *Cosmic Liturgy: The Universe according to Maximus the Confessor*, trans. Brian E. Daley (San Francisco: Ignatius Press, 2003), 57.

[4] "St. Maximus the Confessor between East and West," *Studia Patristica* 32 (1997): 335.

[5] *Bibliotheca hagiographica graeca* (Brussels: Société des Bollandistes, 1909), number 1234.

which paints Maximus as villainous heretic for his stance against Monothelitism.[6] Distilling the facts of Maximus' life is therefore an uncertain process, since the Greek *Vita Maximi* is clearly hagiographical, whereas the Syriac text demonstrates the reverse tendencies. Polycarp Sherwood was the first to devise a chronological arrangement for the entire literary corpus of Maximus the Confessor in 1952, working prior to the discovery of the Syriac *Life of Maximus*. Sherwood's research has since been completely revised by Marek Jankowiak and Phil Booth, and the result of this research is an outline of Maximus' biography that has been commonly accepted in all but several instances.[7]

According to the Greek biographical tradition, Maximus was born into an aristocratic family and studied at Constantinople. The Syriac tradition immediately contradicts this, claiming instead that Maximus was born in Palestine as the son of a Samaritan cloth merchant and a Persian slave girl. Given that Maximus possessed an incredibly refined literary style and was to become the secretary to Emperor Heraclius (reigned AD 610–641), the Greek tradition is far more likely to be accurate on this point. Nevertheless, Phil Booth argued recently for the authenticity of the Syriac tradition that Maximus was born in Palestine, claiming that the internal evidence from Maximus' own writings is not definitive and that Maximus'

[6]Sebastian Brock, "An Early Syriac Life of Maximus the Confessor," *Analecta Bollandiana* (1973): 299–346.

[7]Polycarp Sherwood, *An Annotated Date-List of the Works of Maximus the Confessor* (Rome: Pontificium Institutum S. Anselmi, 1952); Marek Jankowiak and Phil Booth, "A New Date-List of the Works of Maximus the Confessor," in *The Oxford Handbook of Maximus the Confessor*, 19–83, ed. Pauline Allen and Bronwen Neil (Oxford: University Press, 2015). For the basic facts of Maximus' biography, see: Pauline Allen, "Life and Times of Maximus the Confessor," in *The Oxford Handbook of Maximus the Confessor*, ed. Pauline Allen and Bronwen Neil (Oxford: Oxford University Press, 2015), 3–18; Lars Thunberg, *Microcosm and Mediator: The Theological Anthropology of Maximus the Confessor*, second edition (Chicago: Open Court, 1995), 1–7; Andreas N. Stratos, *Byzantium in the Seventh Century*, vol. 3, trans. Harry T. Hionides (Amsterdam: Adolf M. Hakkert, 1975), 119–125. For a historically and theologically detailed review of Maximus' life as well as extensive engagement with the secondary literature, see: Paul M. Blowers, *Maximus the Confessor: Jesus Christ and the Transfiguration of the World* (Oxford: University Press, 2016), 9–63.

connections to the Constantinopolitan court could have been achieved apart from an education in Constantinople.[8]

It was Hereclius who returned the relic of the true cross (reportedly discovered by Constantine's mother, Helena), from the Persians back to Jerusalem in AD 629 or 630. This symbolic act established for him a reputation as a successful military commander and won him favor among the Christian populace in the West.[9] But the politics of the Empire were dramatically altered in the years immediately following, when Muslim invaders captured three of the five Patriarchates—Jerusalem and Antioch in 638, and Alexandria in 642. This new political reality left only Rome and Constantinople as uncontested centers of the Christian world.

At about thirty-five years of age, Maximus left his prestigious post with Heraclius and became a monk at the monastery of Chyrsopolis, located in modern-day Üsküdar, the district of Istanbul lying on the southeastern bank of the Bosporus. Some have seen this conversion to a monastic vocation as a window into Maximus' temperament, revealing that the demands of courtly life were ill-suited to Maximus' uncompromising personality.[10] In 626, an alliance of Avars, Slavs, and Persians besieged Constantinople. There were perhaps eighty thousand men in the allied armies, with the Avars attacking by land from the European side of the Bosporus, the Persians by land from the Asian side, and the Slavs by sea. These massive forces assembled against an estimated twelve thousand men defending Constantinople but failed to capture the city and topple the empire. Constantinople's victory confirmed the loyalty of the

---

[8]Phil Booth, *Crisis of Empire: Doctrine and Dissent at the End of Late Antiquity* (Los Angeles: University of California Press, 2017), 143–155.

[9]Lars Thunberg, *Man and Cosmos: The Vision of St Maximus the Confessor* (Crestwood, NY: St Vladimir's Seminary Press, 1985), 14.

[10]Thunberg can write: "For Maximus, monastic life was never an end in itself. It serves charity, i.e., a double charity toward God and toward one's neighbor. This charity, however, has as a prerequisite an ascetic attitude, which for Maximus included a rather rigorist position concerning doctrine. For that reason, too, all the political and diplomatic compromises of the imperial court became more and more intolerable for him" (ibid., 23).

people to the patriarch of Constantinople, Sergius I, who would become the primary promoter of Monothelitism, or the doctrine that Christ had only one will. During the siege of Constantinople, Maximus left the monastery of Chrysopolis, eventually arriving in Roman North Africa by around 628 and soon thereafter settling in Carthage. Maximus would never again experience peace in the city of Constantinople, but returned in *c.* 654 as a prisoner for his defense of the doctrine of the two wills of Christ. We have very few certain details concerning Maximus' lengthy period of exile in North Africa, but we do have a record of Pyrrhus and Maximus' debate at Carthage in 645, where Maximus persuaded his friend and former patriarch of Constantinople that Christ indeed had two wills.[11] We also know that Maximus traveled to Rome in order to take part in the Lateran Council of 649.

From the details of Maximus' arrest and trial, we can reconstruct with some confidence the following concerning the period of Maximus' sojourn in Roman North Africa.[12] After his arrival in Carthage, Maximus came to settle at the monastery called "Eucratas," where Sophronius was abbot, who was later to become Patriarch of Jerusalem in 634. Maximus and Sophronius developed a close friendship and, deeply influenced by Sophronius, Maximus began to demonstrate himself to be a defender of Chalcedonian orthodoxy against Monophysitism, Monergism, and Monothelitism.[13] The Council of Chalcedon in 451 had defined that Christ had two natures, stating that Christ is "acknowledged in two natures unconfusedly, unchangeably, indivisibly, inseparably." While this definition was not accepted by the Oriental Orthodox or non-Chalcedonian Churches of Egypt, Syria, and the East, and because of the increasing threat of Persian and Muslim invasions in these regions,

[11]PG 91:288–353.

[12]See George Ostrogorsky, *History of the Byzantine* State, trans. Joan Hussey, revised edition (New Brunswick, NJ: Rutgers University Press, 1969), 117–121.

[13]For a full discussion of the controversy, accompanied by a catalogue of the source documents, see Friedhelm Winkelmann, *Der monenergetisch-monotheletische Streit* (Frankfurt am Main: Peter Lang, 2001).

there was increasing political pressure to maintain unity with the non-Chalcedonian Churches. In direct opposition to the Council of Chalcedon, Monophysitism posited that Christ had in fact only one nature; far more subtly, Monergism sidestepped the question of the number of Christ's natures and wills and affirmed that Christ acted with a single operation. Maximus' position—which has sometimes been positively termed Dyotheletism—argues that Christ had two wills. Because Maximus determined that will is a part of nature, and because Christ has two natures according to the Council of Chalcedon, he concluded that it was necessary for Christ to have two wills.[14]

As a way of attempting to bring resolution to the controversy, in 634, Sergius I, Patriarch of Constantinople, issued a *Psephos* (ψῆφος, "decree"), which determined that one should not speak of either one or two operations in Christ but rather of Christ operating in divine and human realities. Maximus approved the *Psephos*, although he requested further clarification on certain points; Honorius I (Bishop of Rome from 625–38) issued a letter of congratulations to the eastern Churches on achieving doctrinal unity.[15] But in fact the dispute had not been resolved. In 638, Emperor Heraclius issued an *Ecthesis* (ἔκθεσις, "public notice"), which repeated the key elements of the

[14]Ian McFarland explains Maximus' concern lucidly: "Over against the Monothelite claim that Christ, as one person or hypostasis, had but one will, Maximus insisted that proper interpretation of the Council of Chalcedon demanded that Christ be confessed as having two wills, corresponding to his existence in two natures. Only so was it possible to honour the venerable principle, 'that which [Christ] has not assumed he has not healed'" (" 'Naturally and by Grace': Maximus the Confessor on the Operation of the Will," *Scottish Journal of Theology* [2005]: 418); see also idem. "The Theology of the Will," *The Oxford Handbook of Maximus the Confessor*, 516–532. McFarland then continues to explain Maximus' reasoning in further arguing that Christ had a *natural* will but not a *gnomic* will. On this further point, see also: Paul M. Blowers, "Maximus the Confessor and John of Damascus on Gnomic Will (γνώμη) in Christ: Clarity and Ambiguity," *Union Seminary Quarterly Review* 63 (2012): 44–50; John Meyendorff, "Free Will (γνώμη) in Maximus the Confessor," in *The Ecumenical World of Orthodox Civilization: Essays in Honor of Georges Florovksy*, 71–75, ed. Andrew Blane (The Hague: Mouton, 1974).

[15]Pauline Allen, "Life and Times of Maximus the Confessor," in *The Oxford Handbook of Maximus the Confessor*, 5.

II. Introduction to *On the Ecclesiastical Mystagogy*

a. *The Mystagogical Tradition in the Early Church*

Maximus the Confessor's treatise is titled Περὶ ἐκκλησιαστικῆς μυσταγωγίας, "On the Ecclesiastical Mystagogy." The term "mystagogy" is simply a transliteration of the Greek word μυσταγωγία and means "initiation into the mysteries." The Greek term μυστήριον (*mystērion*) is translated into Latin as *sacramentum* and may refer to either baptism or the Eucharist. In the fourth century, we have four Church fathers who delivered "mystagogies," or structured lectures on the theology of the sacraments: (1) Cyril of Jerusalem (AD 313–87) in the *Introductory Lectures* (*procatechesis*), *Lenten Lectures* (*catecheses*), and *Mystagogical Lectures* (*catecheses mystagogicae*), (2) Ambrose of Milan (333–97) in *On the Sacraments*, (3) John Chrysostom (349–407) in the *Baptismal Instructions*, and (4) Theodore of Mopsuestia (350–428) in the *Catechetical Homilies*.[18] This proliferation of mystagogies in the fourth century is without precedent in the early Church, and the phenomenon disappears almost as abruptly as it appears. For these authors, the term *mystagogy* refers to an explanation of the faith for those who have newly concluded their catechumenate and have been baptized as Christians at the Easter vigil. For the fourth-century authors, the "catechetical lectures" were delivered to those who were approaching baptism; the "mystagogical lectures" were delivered to those who had recently been baptized. Maximus the Confessor's own language is notably different from the

[18]See the study by Enrico Mazza, *Mystagogy: A Theology of Liturgy in the Patristic Age*, trans. Matthew J. O'Connell (New York: Pueblo, 1989); *The Works of Saint Cyril of Jerusalem*, trans. Leo P. McCauley and Anthony A. Stephenson, Fathers of the Church, vols. 61 and 64 (Washington, DC: Catholic University of America Press, 1969, 1970); the *catecheses mystagogicae* are sometimes attributed to Cyril's successor, John of Jerusalem; Ambrose, *Theological and Dogmatic Works*, trans. Roy J. Deferrari, *Fathers of the Church*, vol. 44 (Washington, DC: Catholic University of America Press, 1963); John Chrysostom, *Baptismal Instructions*, trans. Paul W. Harkins, Ancient Christian Writers, vol. 31 (Westminster: Newman Press, 1963); Theodore of Mopsuestia, *Commentary on the Lord's Prayer, and on the Sacraments of Baptism and the Eucharist*, trans. Alphonse Mingana (Cambridge: Heffer, 1933).

authors above; he appears to use the word "mystagogy" simply as a synonym for the Divine Liturgy.[19]

The mystagogical lectures of the fourth century are outlined most completely in the lectures traditionally ascribed to Cyril of Jerusalem. Cyril informs his catechumens about what they can expect to learn in the mystagogical lectures that he would deliver in the Church of the Holy Sepulchre in Jerusalem in the week following Easter:

> After Easter's holy day of salvation, you will come every day, starting Monday, immediately after the assembly into the holy place of the Resurrection, where, God willing, you will hear other lectures. In these you will be instructed again in the reasons for everything that has been done, reasons warranted by proofs from the Old and the New Testaments; first concerning what is done immediately before Baptism; then how you were cleansed by the Lord "in the bath of water by means of the word" [Eph 5.26]; how like priests you have become partakers of the name of Christ; and how the seal of the fellowship of the Holy Spirit has been given to you. You will be instructed concerning the mysteries at the altar of the New Testament, those mysteries first instituted here in Jerusalem. You will hear what the Sacred Scriptures have delivered to us, and of the efficacy of these mysteries; how you must approach them, when and how to receive them; and last of all, how you must behave in word and deed worthily of the grace received, that all of you may be able to enjoy life everlasting. These points will, God willing, be the burden of our talks.[20]

When one compares Maximus' *On the Ecclesiastical Mystagogy* with the mystagogical lectures of the fourth century, one immediately notes several critical differences. First, whereas the mystagogical

---

[19]See Maximus the Confessor, O*n the Ecclesiastical Mystagogy* 2.

[20]Cyril of Jerusalem, *Catechetical Homilies* 18.33 (*The Works of Saint Cyril of Jerusalem*, trans. Leo P. McCauley and Anthony A. Stephenson [Washington, DC: The Catholic University of America Press, 1970]), 138.

lectures of Cyril, Ambrose, Chrysostom, and Theodore were clearly delivered to those who had recently been baptized, the historical context of Maximus' treatise is neither stated nor important for the interpretation of the treatise. Second, whereas the mystagogical lectures of Cyril, Ambrose, Chrysostom, and Theodore read like their sermons, Maximus' *On the Ecclesiastical Mystagogy* can scarcely be conceived of as a set of homilies. In the mystagogical literature of the fourth century, we find direct address to the audience, abundant illustrations, moral directives, and rhetorical flourishes, and all of these features indicate a style that is intended to be engaging and memorable for live audiences. By contrast, the philosophical sophistication, terminological precision, and intricacy of argument we find in the *On the Ecclesiastical Mystagogy* clearly reveals that Maximus' series of meditations is intended to be read and reread in reflective silence. Third, there is also a notable difference between Maximus' use of Scripture and that of the fourth-century mystagogical literature. Whereas Cyril, Ambrose, Chrysostom, and Theodore attempt to explain the sacraments in the light of an allegorical reading of Scripture, Maximus' aim is to interpret the sacraments as framed by ultimate reality—a metaphysical or "cosmological" reading of the sacraments. Whereas the fourth-century authors weave a constant stream of Scriptures into their sermons, Maximus is decidedly more placid in his appeals to Scripture. When elucidating the significance of the white robes donned by the newly baptized, for example, Ambrose expounds the symbols from the Pentateuch and the other Old Testament books that foreshadow the putting off of sin and the putting on of the righteousness of Christ.[21] Maximus cites the Scripture characteristically not in order to support a specific argument but rather to unfold a new aspect of a meditation that he has already set up, and he only occasionally places the focus of his attention to the exposition of the Scripture.

[21] Ambrose, *On the Mysteries* 7 (Deferrari, 17).

b. Outline of the Ecclesiastical Mystagogy:

Maximus' treatise is essentially a commentary on the liturgy. In this concise text, Maximus walks step by step through the liturgy, explaining the theological significance of each element in detail. We find a number of commentaries on the liturgy following Maximsus' in the seventh century and beyond, but *On the Ecclesiastical Mystagogy* stands as the first.[22] Subsequent commentaries on the liturgy demonstrate an indebtedness to Maximus', and this influence is still clearly traceable by the time of the late Byzantine theologians Nicolas Cabasilas (d. 1392) and Symeon of Thessalonica (d. 1429).[23]

The *Ecclesiastical Mystagogy* comprises a preface, twenty-four chapters of varying lengths, a summary, and a conclusion, but the complete work divides into two basic parts. The first part is a series of reflections on the nature of the Church. Maximus first establishes that the Church represents the image of God. Maximus then establishes that the Church represents the entire created order in a cascading sequence of analogies: the Church reflects the universe (comprising both intelligible and sensible realms), the sensible realm of the universe alone, man (comprising both body and soul), and the soul of man alone. In the second part, Maximus examines the symbolic significance of the various elements of the liturgy in three cycles. In the first cycle (chapters 8–21), Maximus offers a theological interpretation for the elements of the liturgy in the following order: (I) the entrance of the bishop into the Church, (II) the entrance of the people into the Church, (III) the first reading from the Scriptures, (IV) the singing of hymns, (V) the pronouncement of peace, (VI) the reading of the Gospel, (VII) the closing of the doors of the Church, (VIII) the entrance of Eucharistic elements, (IX) the exchange of the kiss of peace, (X) the recitation of the Nicene

---

[22]René Bornert, *Les commentaires byzantins de la divine liturgie du VIIe au XVe siècle* (Paris: Institut Français d'Études Byzantines, 1966), 83.

[23]Nicolaus Cabasilas, *A Commentary on the Divine Liturgy*, trans. J. M. Hussey and P. A. McNulty (Crestwood, NY: St. Vladimir's Press, 2010); Symeon of Thessalonica, *The Liturgical Commentaries*, trans. Steven Hawkes-Teeples (Toronto: Pontifical Institute of Medieval Studies, 2011).

Creed, (XI) the singing of the "Trisagion" ("Holy, Holy, Holy"), (XII) the praying of the Lord's Prayer, and (XIII) the singing of the "One is Holy" and concluding hymns. In the second cycle (chapter 23), Maximus examines the symbolic significance of the various components of the liturgy for a second time, this time in relation to the soul, by which the liturgy is perceived to be the journey of the soul to union with God. Finally, in the third cycle (chapter 24), Maximus again examines the components of the liturgy, this time from the standpoint of the illumination of the grace of the Holy Spirit, by which we see the moral transformation that each component of the liturgy effects.[24]

In the preface, Maximus explains to the reader that Theocharistos (concerning whom we know nothing) requested that he write out his theological reflections on the liturgy. Expressing reluctance and a sense of inadequacy for the task, Maximus nevertheless affirms his willingness to fulfill the request, citing the sources to whom the treatise will be indebted: the "blessed elder" (who remains anonymous throughout the treatise but whom scholars surmise to be Sophronius

[24]In chapter 23, Maximus does not explicitly name each of these components enumerated above, but he outlines the liturgy in essentially the same order. In chapter 24, Maximus differs only very slightly from the order listed above in that (a) he speaks only of a first entrance as the first component, not differentiating between a first entrance of the bishop and a first entrance of the people, and (b) he does not mention the pronouncement of peace. According to the Liturgy of Saint John Chrysostom, the order of service is: (I) the Enarxis, (II) the little entrance (i.e., entrance of the Holy Gospel), (III) the lesson, (IV) the common prayers, (V) dismissal of the catechumens, (VI) the prayers of the faithful, (VII) the offertory, (VIII) the kiss of peace, (IX) the creed, (X) the anaphora, (XI) communion, (XII) dismissal (The Stavopegic Monastery of St. John the Baptist, *The Orthodox Liturgy* [Oxford: University Press, 1982]). The order of the liturgy according to Maximus is significantly different from the order presented in Cyril of Jerusalem's mystagogical lectures, which is the most developed from among the fourth-century authors. By way of contrast, Cyril discusses the liturgy in the following order: (I) baptism, (II) the anointing with oil, (III) the washing of hands, (IV) the kiss, (V) "lift up your hearts," (VI) the singing of the "Trisagion" ("Holy, Holy, Holy"), (VII) the consecration of the Eucharist, (VIII) prayers of intercession, (IX) the Lord's Prayer, (X) the celebration of the Eucharist. Andrew Louth can write of the Byzantine liturgical tradition: "And if it is true that [it] . . . is not much studied, that is at least in part because there are better things to do with it than subject it to scholarly scrutiny" ("Between East and West," 344).

of Jerusalem)[25] and Dionysius the Areopagite (an author who identifies himself as the first-century convert of the Apostle Paul mentioned in Acts 17.34, but whom modern scholarship refers to as Pseudo-Dionysius and identifies as a pseudonymous author of a corpus of fifth or sixth-century theological treatises).[26] Maximus expresses warm admiration for the blessed elder, whose life of ascetic discipline Maximus had apparently witnessed personally. As his final statement in the preface, Maximus affirms that God alone can assure the truthfulness of what he is about to write, because God alone is the truth reflected in the mind that is reflecting truthfully. Maximus then expands on this paradox, delivering one of the most striking expositions of the apophatic theological method in patristic literature.[27]

In the first three chapters of *On the Ecclesiastical Mystagogy*, Maximus establishes that the Church reflects God; the Church unites the intelligible and the sensible realm in a way that reflects the creative act of God at the beginning of the world. God united the

---

[25]Irénée-Henri Dalmais, "Mystère liturgique et divinisation dans la *Mystagogie de saint Maxime le Confesseur*," in *Epektasis: Mélanges patristiques offerts au Cardinal Jean Daniélou*, ed. Jacques Fontaine and Charles Kannengiesser (Paris: Beauchesne, 1972), 55–56.

[26]Hypatius of Ephesus contested the authorship of the Pseudo-Dionysius corpus as early as AD 532, claiming that the documents were in fact written by the Severians in order to support Monophysitism. Despite these accusations, the theologians of the medieval period welcomed these writings as from the pen of Paul's first-century convert, and it was not until Lorenzo Valla uncovered clear dependence on the Neo-Platonist Proclus (d. AD 485) that the pseudonymity of the author was generally recognized. Hubertus Drobner concludes concerning the historical identity of Pseudo-Dionysius: "Probably [he] was a Syrian Christian who had been living in Athens for a long time, where, as is well known, a circle of Syrian scholars gathered near the end of the fifth century." *The Fathers of the Church: A Comprehensive Introduction*, trans. Siegfried S. Schatzmann, ed. William Harmless, S.J. (Peabody, MA: Henrickson, 2007), 533.

[27]In explaining what apophatic theology is, Met. Kallistos Ware quotes the words of Cardinal Newman that apophatic theology is continually "saying and unsaying to a positive effect" (*The Orthodox Way*, revised edition [Crestwood: St Vladimir's Seminary Press, 1995], 14). Ware then continues: "Having made an assertion about God, we must pass beyond it: the statement is not untrue, yet neither it nor any other form of words can contain the fullness of the transcendent God."

sensible and the intelligible realms at the creation when he infused physical materials with spiritual meaning. The Church mirrors this when she displays spiritual mysteries in the elements of the bread and wine of the Eucharist, or the water and oil of baptism and anointing, or the music and drama of the singing and reading of Scripture. As comprised of nave and sanctuary, the Church exhibits the interrelationship of the sensible and intelligible realms of the cosmos in bringing together yet maintaining separation between the congregants and the divine mysteries. Maximus argues that in fact all things reveal God's loving nature in some aspect or another. Everything that exists discloses God as its ultimate cause; nothing that is can conceal the imprint of the creativity and power of God. God is the oneness that gives unity to the many, and so the Church is to unite the disparate factions of alienated humanity into the one people of God.

In chapters four and five, Maximus draws analogies between the Church and man and between the Church and the soul of man. Maximus explores how the Church (comprised of sanctuary, altar, and nave) is analogous to man (who is soul, mind, and body), relating the spiritual disciplines practiced by each part of man to the spiritual life centered in each part of the Church. In chapter five, Maximus demonstrates that the Church is also analogous to the soul alone, and this is probably the most technical section of the entire treatise. Toward the conclusion of chapter five, Maximus introduces theosis, a theme that Maximus explicitly names infrequently but which controls the whole shape of his theology. Theosis—that is, union with God or becoming one with God—is the ultimate goal of all spiritual progress; the journey that Maximus describes in his meditations on the liturgy finds its end in the rapturous and eternal union with God. Every element of the Church's liturgy is to bring the worshiper into greater union with God. In order to make sense of the mystery of theosis, Maximus appeals to the analogy of the intimacy of marital union and affirms that God will become "one flesh" and "one spirit"

with the Church and with the soul, invoking Paul's teaching from 1 Corinthians 6.16–17 and Ephesians 5.31–32.

It is at this point in Maximus' argument that he introduces the link between the *Logos* (Λόγος) and the *logoi* (λόγοι), a relationship that is fundamental to understanding the theology of theosis. Maximus uses the term λόγος in a variety of senses, including "word," "discourse," "reason," and "principle," and his use of this term and our translation require some explanation. In light of the diversity of senses with which Maximus infuses the term, we have primarily translated λόγοι as "principles" in this edition of *On the Ecclesiastical Mystagogy*, supplying other translations where necessary. We considered the possibility of simply transliterating the Greek λόγος into English as *logos*, but we chose ultimately not to do this, since for Maximus λόγος is a common word, and therefore it seemed to us that it would distort our translation to introduce a philosophical technical term for λόγος. To Maximus, the word λόγος was perfectly mundane—as mundane as the word "word"—and therefore the term correctly brings with it the expectation that God's revelatory principles would be found throughout all of reality in the perceptible world.[28]

In weaving the concept of the λόγος into his theology, Maximus is heir to the older tradition from the Gospel of John and Neo-platonic philosophy, but Maximus develops the concept far beyond the

[28]The Greek word λόγος is renowned for its wide semantic field. A survey of the English equivalents for λόγος from Liddell, Scott, and Jones' *Greek-English Lexicon* includes: "account, analogy, argument, assertion, audit, branch, case, computation, conscience, consideration, correspondence, debate, definition, deliberation, department, description, dialogue, discourse, discussion, division, esteem, event, explanation, expression, fame, fiction, formula, function, ground, honor, hypothesis, idea, language, law, legend, matter, maxim, measure, mention, message, narrative, notice, oracle, oration, order, phrase, plan, plea, plot, point, praise, precept, pretense, pretext, principle, proof, proportion, proposition, prose, proverb, question, quibble, ratio, reason, reasoning, reckoning, reflection, relation, report, reputation, rule, rumor, saying, section, sentence, speech, story, subject, sum, tale, talk, term, thesis, tidings, thinking, total, treatise, tradition, utterance, value, word, worth, and whim." In other words, according to the standard Greek dictionary, λόγος can be translated into English with words that begin with every letter of the alphabet except j, k, x, y, and z!

framework of the meaning of the word λόγος that could be reconstructed from these sources alone.[29] In essence, the λόγοι are that which is intelligible in the sensible realm. That is, the λόγοι are what give meaning to the material reality that we experience. Perceived by the mind rather than the senses, the λόγοι are reflections of the divine Λόγος, and therefore in contemplation the λόγοι refer us ever onward to God: "When the mind perceives in contemplation the principles [λόγοι] of the things that are, it will end in God himself, as the cause and beginning and end of the creation and origin and as the everlasting foundation of the compass of the whole universe."[30] The λόγοι then are at the heart of Maximus' entire worldview. Throughout the treatise, Maximus' recurring theme is the interwovenness of the cosmic and the mundane, the eternal and the present, the intelligible and the sensible: "For the whole intelligible realm, which is impressed mystically in symbolic forms in the whole sensible realm, appears for those who are able to see, and the whole sensible realm, which is intellectually simplified into its principles [λόγοι] according to the mind, exists in the whole intelligible realm."[31] The λόγοι are the elements that render communion between the intellectual realm and the sensible realm—and, ultimately, union between the divine and human—possible.

At the core of the meaning of the term λόγος is the concept of "significance"; that is, the referent toward which communication or intellection points. Christos Yannaras writes penetratingly: "λόγος is the mode by which everything that is becomes manifest, becomes known."[32] The various meanings denoted by the word λόγος center on the concept of "disclosure," Sotiris Mitralexis observes, and thus

[29]See Andrew Louth, "St Maximos' Doctrine of the logoi of Creation," *Studia Patristica* 48 (2010): 77–84; Sotiris Mitralexis, "Maximus' 'Logical' Ontology: An Introduction and Interpretive Approach to Maximus the Confessor's Notion of the λόγοι," *Sobornost* 37 (2015): 65–82.

[30]*Ecclesiastical Mystagogy* 1.

[31]Ibid., 2.

[32]*Σχεδίασμα εἰσαγωγῆς στὴ φιλοσοφία* (Athens: Domos, 1988), 20; quoted in Mitralexis, "Maximus' 'Logical' Ontology: An Introduction and Interpretive Approach to Maximus the Confessor's Notion of the λόγοι," 69.

the word becomes in Christian theology a key term for the revelation of God in the person of his Son Jesus Christ. The λόγοι—that is, the intelligible elements within the realm of experience—inevitably refer back to God, the Creator who has infused his creation with purpose and meaning.[33] As Maximus unfolds his argument in *On the Ecclesiastical Mystagogy*, it is clear that for him this is not merely an abstract theological principle but an entirely practical element, for the relationship between God and creation articulated in the theology of the Λόγος and the λόγοι allows Maximus to discover God in everything. The λόγοι are united in the Λόγος, God the Word, and therefore as we perceive the λόγοι in contemplation, we are drawn into union with God.[34] Maximus concludes chapter five:

> So then, because the soul 'becomes one' in this fashion and is brought together to itself and to God, there will be no reason [λόγος] to further divide the soul conceptually into many parts; the soul has been crowned as the head by the first, only, and one God the Word [lit. "Word and God," Λόγῳ καὶ θεῷ]. All the principles [λόγοι] of everything that exists are and subsist singly in Him according to one unintelligible simplicity, since he is the creator and maker of everything that exists.[35]

After demonstrating that the same comparison between the Church and a man can also be drawn between the Scripture (which is

[33]Mitralexis can write: "The attempt to contemplate the λόγος of something is the attempt to discover it not as an object, but as God's creation, and, as such as the actualization or disclosure of one's relationship with God" (ibid., 75).

[34]Maximus explains the spiritual significance of what is taking place in the liturgy when the congregants sing the "One is Holy" by again alluding to this process: "When by knowledge they have passed through all the principles [λόγοι] in the things that exist, next the word leads them to the unknowable Monad in an unknowable way" (ibid., 13). See John Zizioulas's exposition of Maximus' understanding of the relationship of the *Logos* and the *logoi*: *Communion and Otherness: Further Studies in Personhood and the Church*, ed. Paul McPartlan (London: T&T Clark, 2006), 66.

[35]*Mystagogy* 5. For Maximus, it is precisely this theology of the relationship of the Λόγος and the λόγοι that makes sense of the incarnation and its corollary—theosis. This link between the incarnation and theosis is exposited by many of the early Church Fathers.

letter and spirit) and a man (who is body and soul) in chapter six, and between the universe (which is composed of sensible and intelligible realms) and a man in chapter seven, Maximus then commences the first cycle of his explanation of the elements of the liturgy (chapters 8–21). The entrance of the priest into the nave represents the incarnation of Christ; the return of the priest to the sanctuary represents the ascension of Christ. The entrance of the people into the Church represents conversion, the reading of Scripture foreshadows the commandments of the Lord for the Christian, and the singing of hymns speaks of the awakening of the soul to the pleasures of life in God. The pronouncement of peace symbolizes the protection of the angels, the reading of the Gospel represents the call to discipleship, the closing of the doors stands for the shutting out of worldliness, the sacrifice of Christ on the cross is the archetype of the celebration of the Eucharist, the kiss of peace typifies the unanimity and bliss of the eternal state, the recitation of the creed adumbrates "the mystical Eucharist that shall be in the age to come,"[36] the singing of the Trisagion foretells the participation of the redeemed with angelic choirs in the worship of God, the Lord's Prayer represents the adoption by God of those who are saved, and the hymns that conclude the liturgy prefigure the joy of heaven. In the second cycle (chapter 23) of his reflections on the elements of the liturgy, Maximus explores the significance of the liturgy for Christian teaching, concluding his exposition with a profound reflection on the doctrine of the Trinity. Maximus then charts a third and final course through the elements of the liturgy (chapter 24), explaining the moral transformation that the Holy Spirit works by grace in the soul of the Christian in each element. In the summary, Maximus exhorts the reader to attend the liturgy faithfully, and in the conclusion, Maximus pleads for clemency for any deficiencies that may remain in the treatise.

[36]*Ecclesiastical Mystagogy* 18.

c. The Ecclesiology of On the Ecclesiastical Mystagogy:

The *Ecclesiastical Mystagogy* is not a systematic exposition of ecclesiology, and yet, in interpreting the meaning of the liturgy celebrated in the Church, Maximus reveals the framework for his theology concerning the nature of the Church. The first principle that Maximus sets out in the text is that the Church represents the image of God.[37] Maximus quotes the scriptural teaching that man is created in the image of God from Genesis 1.26–27 in chapters 4 and 6 of his treatise, but he does not appeal to this biblical reference when he argues that the Church represents the image of God at the beginning of his book. Maximus' argument that the Church represents the image of God is that the Church is analogous to a man and therefore that the Church is also in the image of God. Citing the "blessed elder," Maximus affirms that "the holy Church bears the representation and image of God because she possesses the same activity as him according to imitation and representation."[38] As Maximus then explains, this activity that the Church shares with God is to create unity from division.

The operating principle in Maximus' reflections on the nature of the Church is that the Church represents the image of God, and the most basic principle in Maximus' reflections on the nature of God is that God is known to us as the creator of all that exists. Maximus is not concerned to construct reasons to justify the existence of God. Quite the opposite, Maximus' entry point into theological knowledge is that God as creator of everything that exists can be known in everything because his creativity is reflected in everything that exists, but at the same time God remains unknowable because God as creator is wholly other than everything that exists in the created order. Maximus derives from this paradox that because God is the cause of everything that exists, everything exists in relationship to God: "For as God made all things by his infinite power and brought them into existence, so now he sustains them and draws them together

[37] *Ecclesiastical Mystagogy* 1.
[38] Ibid.

and defines their limits."[39] It is God alone as creator who sustains relationship to everything that exists, and therefore it is God alone to whom everything that exists relates and through whom everything experiences unity. This unity of all things, however, is not a present reality but rather a potential that God continues to actualize as he unfolds his redemptive purposes in and through the Church. This is what Maximus means when he says that the Church is in the image of God "because she possesses the same activity as his according to imitation and representation."[40] The Church is God's agent to bring about unity—unity among divided peoples in an immediate sense and unity throughout the cosmos in an ultimate sense.

One more distinction must be established before the logic of Maximus' ecclesiology can be properly framed, and that is the priority of the relationship between God and creation over relationships between created beings. Because all of creation exists in relationship to God, every part of the created order also exists in relationship to every other part of the created order. The relationship between created beings is rendered secondary or subordinate in some way to the relationship that God sustains with his creation as creator, but the relationship between created beings does not cease. Maximus articulates this principle most clearly when he affirms that the relationship between God and creation "nullifies and covers over" every relationship between created beings, but that this is "not because it corrupts and destroys them and causes them not to be, but because it surpasses and outshines them."[41] Maximus offers a concluding analogy: "As the sun is more brilliant than the stars in nature and power, so also its appearance covers over them as a cause does its effects."[42]

The unity that God causes to exist between himself and his creation is therefore not a unity that causes the individuality of the constituent parts of creation to be lost or destroyed; creation rather

[39]Ibid.
[40]Ibid.
[41]Ibid.
[42]Ibid.

comes to experience the very unity of the person of God, which as
Chalcedon proclaims is a unity in which both oneness and distinction are maintained. Maximus elucidates:

> Because he possesses full command of everything around him
> as their cause, beginning, and end, he makes the things that
> have been set apart from one another by nature to be the things
> that have converged with one another by the one power of their
> relationship with him as their beginning. And it is by this power
> that all things are led to an identity of movement and existence
> that is indistinguishable and without confusion.[43]

Chalcedon decreed that Christ is "to be acknowledged in two
natures, inconfusedly, unchangeably, indivisibly, inseparably; the
distinction of natures being by no means taken away by the union
[ἐν δύο φύσεσιν, ἀσυγχύτως, ἀτρέπτως, ἀδιαιρέτως, ἀχωρίστως
γνωριζόμενον· οὐδαμοῦ τῆς τῶν φύσεων διαφορᾶς ἀνηρημένης
διὰ τὴν ἔνωσιν]."[44] Christ possesses two natures, one human and
one divine, but the distinctness of natures does not preclude the
unity of Christ's person as the second member of the Trinity. This
foundational theological insight assures Maximus that division in
the Church—and Maximus, who would be accused of collaborating
with the Bishop of Rome and so conspiring against the Patriarch of
Constantinople, experienced in an intimate way the pain of division
in the Church—does not threaten or overrule the unity that God
grants in and through the Church for the world.

For Maximus, the Church is the place where God's grace unifies
humanity because the Church is the place where God brings humanity into union with himself. Maximus writes:

> For, from among men, women, and children, nearly bound-
> less in number, who are many in race and class and nation and
> language and occupation and age and persuasion and trade and
> manners and customs and pursuits, and again, those who are

[43]Ibid.
[44]Philip Schaff, *Creeds of Christendom* (New York: Harper, 1877), 2:62.

divided and most different from one another in expertise and worth and fortune and features and habits, those who are in the holy Church and are regenerated by her and are recreated by the Spirit—to all he gives equally and grants freely one divine form and designation, that is to be and to be called from Christ. And he gives according to faith the one simple, indivisible, and undivided relationship, which does not allow the many and unspeakable differences about each one—even if they exist—to be known on account of the universal reference and union of all the people in the Church.[45]

Maximus does not sidestep the innumerable differences between people and societies or the severity of these differences, but his comprehension of who God is gives him a breathtaking confidence in the institution of the Church. If God is to effect his plan of redemption at all, then the divisions in the Church do not cancel the work of God, but God who works to bring his grace to the world in and through the Church overcomes the divisions between created beings by his relationship to all of creation as the creator. In order to render it impossible for us to fail to see the implications of his mystical theology for ecclesiology, at the end of the treatise Maximus reiterates that the Church is by definition the community in and by which God accomplishes his mission of reconciling the world to himself:

Therefore, the holy Church is a representation and image of God, as it has been said above, because the unconfused oneness, which she works according to God's boundless power and wisdom from the different substances of the things that exist, God works as creator and the one who holds all things together by holding all things to himself as their summit.

This principle, that the Church as the community of the redeemed experiences unity with God, leads Maximus to articulate his doctrine of theosis. Maximus is careful to specify that the unity that the Church experiences with and in God is not a unity of nature.

[45] Ibid.

We should therefore not expect that the Church will somehow become an addition to the three persons of the Trinity when theosis is achieved in the eternal state and the Church becomes one with God. In the preface to his treatise, Maximus states in the strongest possible language the transcendence of God in his nature: "He neither in any way whatsoever belongs to nor comes to belong to the things that are or that are becoming, whose essence he constitutes. He is by nature in the same class as absolutely nothing of the things that are."[46] Maximus adheres to this line of reasoning so strictly that he concludes that we may affirm properly that God does not exist, since God entirely transcends being. In his meditation on apophatic theology in the preface, the final point for Maximus is that God in his nature cannot be united with anything from the created order: "For nothing at all—whether it exists or does not exist—is united with him by nature because he is their cause."[47]

But if God the creator cannot be joined to creation in his nature, the warp and woof of Maximus' mystical theology is that God by his grace unites himself to the Church. The consequences of this conclusion for the contemporary ecumenical discussion are profound. How shall we conceive of Christian unity today if the Church is by definition the place where God achieves unity between himself and humanity and this unity between God and creation subordinates divisions between created beings? Maximus' theology of Christian unity can surely teach us as much as his own personal example of faithfulness in the face of astonishing failure and division.

---

[46]Ibid., pref.

[47]Ibid. It worth noting that, when the biblical author states that the redeemed become "partakers of the divine nature [θείας κοινωνοὶ φύσεως]" (2 Pet 1.4), the term "nature" is not synchronized with Maximus' use of the term. Maximus affirms that nothing in the created order can become one with God's nature as creator; the biblical author's point is that the knowledge of God brings about the practice of virtue, and that the redeemed therefore begin to emulate God's own holiness.

d. *The Cosmological Dimensions of the* Ecclesiastical Mystagogy:

After Maximus establishes that the Church is in the image of God, the second foundational teaching that he draws from the "blessed elder" is that the Church "is a representation and image of the entire universe, which subsists in visible and invisible realities, because the Church contains the same oneness and diversity as God."[48] As Maximus exposits his doctrine of the Church, he explains that, because the Church is in the image of God, the liturgy functions as a map to the entire universe. It is in this aspect that we may refer to Maximus' theology as "cosmological" in its orientation and connotations. The Church is in the image of God because the elements of the Church's worship encompass in a complete form both the intellectual and the sensible realms. Maximus begins this part of the treatise by working through the floorplan of the Church: there is the sanctuary (which is reserved for the clergy) and the nave (where the congregation assembles for public worship). But this division in the structure of the Church does not mean that the Church is somehow divided spiritually or not a unified entity. Maximus argues that the Church "displays that both the sanctuary and the nave are identical to one another and illustrates that each one exists in the other according to exchange."[49] Maximus then goes on to explain that, on the one hand, "the nave is identical to the sanctuary according to power,"[50] because the Eucharist sanctifies the nave. On the other hand, "the sanctuary is identical to the nave according to activity," Maximus continues to explain, "because it is the place where the never-ending mystagogy begins."[51] These phrases, "according to power" and "according to activity" are repeated throughout the treatise, as Maximus divides all of reality into potentiality and actuality, the transcendent and the immanent, the creator and creation.

[48]Ibid., 2.
[49]Ibid.
[50]Ibid.
[51]Ibid.

What generates a possibly infinite complexity for Maximus' understanding of the cosmos is that these two realms (potentiality and actuality) are not finally perfectly separable, and it is this linked status that transposes Maximus' theological reflections to a genuinely "mystical" state. The created order is divided into the "intelligible realm" (which correlates to potentiality or that which is immaterial and can be known only by the soul) and the "sensible realm" (which correlates to actuality and that which is material and can be known by the senses). These levels of reality are completely distinguishable from one another but overlap, and therefore there emerges an intense complexity to human experience which theoretically allows for an experience of God in any part of reality. One could say that Maximus' view of the intelligible realm and the sensible realm is that they are interpenetrating, although Maximus does not use this word; Maximus' own term is "ingeniously interwoven"—language that is evocative of the union of Christ in two natures—and so we see once more that Maximus' mysterious, cosmological theology is anchored in the christology of Chalcedon. Maximus can state that "the entire universe . . . is seen in wisdom through this Church that is made with hands."[52]

Having completed his meditation on how the Church reflects the image of the universe, Maximus outlines how the Church reflects the image of the soul. In doing so, Maximus demonstrates the mystical potential of his reflections, in showing how the interrelationship of two subjects (i.e., the Church and the universe) can also be modeled within the interrelationship of the first subject (i.e., the Church) and a subset of the second subject (i.e., the soul). This exposition takes place in chapter five of the *Ecclesiastical Mystagogy*, and this chapter is considerably lengthier than the other chapters in the treatise and demonstrates the capacity of Maximus' theological system for intricacy and mystery.

Maximus first divides the soul into the intellectual power and the animate power, the former being the part of the soul that is

[52]Ibid.

directed by the will, and the latter being that part that remains unaffected by the will. Maximus then further subdivides intellectual power into the contemplative part (which he calls the mind) and the practical power (which he calls reason). Maximus then explains the functions of each of these parts: "The mind is the part that causes motion in the intellectual power, while the reason is the part that is provident in the animate power."[53] Maximus' logic seems straightforward enough: there is a contemplative and a practical function in the operations of the soul, and the contemplative part drives the intellectual power, and the practical part drives the animate power. However, if we attempt to diagram Maximus' verbal depiction of the soul on a whiteboard, we quickly realize from the tangle of lines that results that we have misunderstood some key aspect of his analysis. Maximus indicates that the reason and the mind are components of the intellectual power, but his next step is to define reason as a component of the animate power. Which is which? Is reason a part of the intellectual power or a part of the animate power? Our basic error is to assume that Maximus analyzes the soul as one might dissect an organ of the human body—separating one part from another. However, for Maximus, drawing distinctions between the various components of the soul does not divide one part from another because the soul encompasses interpenetrating realities. Perhaps we could chart out Maximus' logic best by saying that the various components of the soul are simultaneously parts and functions. It may be helpful to imagine that Maximus' theological vision of the cosmos anticipates quantum physics, whereby material reality is described as both particles and waves. When we understand that Maximus oscillates between describing the various aspects of the soul as parts and functions, we begin to be able to follow his logic. This freedom to float between part and function in his analysis of the soul creates a potentially infinite complexity in Maximus' system. But, in his exploration of all of the relationships that are generated

[53]Ibid., 5.

from these dynamics, Maximus' purpose remains to trace each relationship back to God.

Maximus says that the soul has two major functions, that of the
intellectual power and that of the animate power. The intellectual
power has two components: the mind and reason, and the mind
functions within the intellectual power, whereas reason functions
within the animate power. When the mind keeps itself entirely
oriented toward God, it may be called wisdom. Maximus uses the
phrase "it is and is called" wisdom to refer the state of the mind when
it completely fulfills its potential. Maximus then goes on to expli-
cate the relationships possible for reason, but instead of outlining
a parallel set of relationships (i.e., when reason keeps itself entirely
oriented toward God), Maximus begins an arduous progression in
the opposite direction. Maximus states that reason "is and is called"
prudence when it drives the animate power to reflect God to an
equal degree as the mind by the practice of virtue. The mind arrives
at truth and reason arrives at the good through the practice of virtue.
In demonstrating the capacity for interpenetration of all parts of the
soul, Maximus is able to conclude that both the contemplative and
the practical life arrive equally upon true knowledge of God: "From
both the mind and reason, true expertise of divine and human realities unite, a knowledge which is actually infallible knowledge and
the end of every divine philosophy according to the Christians."[54]
Harnessing the power of paradox and the mechanism of interpenetration, Maximus' mystical theology generates a potentially
infinite complexity, and therefore Maximus can never complete the
diagrams that he begins. He can only chart out one possible set of
relationships, and the inevitable result of his reflection on any particular set of relationships is to arrive upon God.

When Maximus approaches the discussion of the individual elements of the liturgy, the cosmological dimensions of his theological
system come into clear focus. The elements of the liturgy are both
parts of material reality and functions of divine grace. Maximus

[54]Ibid.

walks through every aspect of the liturgy, explaining, in its first aspect, that the entrance of the priest into the Church "bears the representation and image" of the first advent of the Savior.[55] Maximus' language varies concerning the intensity of the association between the physical performance of the liturgy and the spiritual reality. In his opening reflections, he speaks of the correspondence simply in terms of "representation and image." Maximus states that the ascension of Christ is "symbolically represented" in the bishop's taking his seat at the front of the Church.[56] The entrance of the people with the priest into the Church "signifies" and "indicates" Christian conversion, and the reading of Scripture "points toward" the revealing of God's purposes for the lives of the Christians. The singing of hymns "indicates" the awakening of the soul to delight in God, as the kiss of peace does "the divine acceptance conveyed by the holy angels."[57]

However, as we progress further into Maximus' depiction of the liturgy, the lines between represented reality and actual reality become blurred. Maximus says that the reading of the Gospels "introduces" the suffering of the faithful on behalf of the word.[58] We see the light of divine reality shine through the elements of the liturgy yet more brilliantly as Maximus writes concerning the people: "Then the word counts them among the angels through the Trisagion."[59] It is not simply that in singing the Trisagion the people echo angelic choirs or that what is happening in the Church mirrors what is happening in celestial courts. No, the people are "counted among the angels." From this point onward Maximus' language describing the elements of the liturgy continues in a strain not of mere symbolism but of real spiritual participation:

> The word brings them to God the Father because they have been adopted in the Spirit through the prayer through which

[55]Ibid., 8.
[56]Ibid.
[57]Ibid., 12.
[58]Ibid., 13.
[59]Ibid.

they are deemed worthy to call God "Father." And from there, when by knowledge they have passed through all the principles in the things that exist, next the word leads them to the unknowable Monad in an unknowable way through the singing of the "One Is Holy." And they are deified by grace and made like the undivided identity by participation with the Monad to the best of their ability.[60]

In the chapters that immediately follow, Maximus then reverts to speaking of the various elements of the liturgy as symbolizing spiritual reality, using terms like "foreshadows," "prefigures," "portrays," "foretells," and "intimates."

In the final chapter of the treatise, it is evident once again that the elements of the liturgy are no mere symbolic representations, but it is also clear that the definitive experience of spiritual reality awaits us beyond this life when we will receive "the archetypical mysteries that are represented here through sensible symbols."[61] Maximus reviews each of the elements of the liturgy one final time. In the original Greek, this chapter is comprised of one extraordinarily long sentence, which means that each of the English sentences in our translation of this chapter is a single clause in this enormous sentence. In order to render these Greek clauses as complete English sentences, our translation team was required to reinsert the subject ("grace") and a verb ("brings about") into each sentence, as for example: "Through the Trisagion, grace brings about oneness with the angels."[62] However, the marvelous ways of Greek grammar allow Maximus to presume the subject and verb, leaving only two phrases—one stating the part of the liturgy and the other stating the spiritual reality—standing juxtaposed. The implication is clear. Maximus ends this final chapter by reaffirming that because the conclusion of grace in our lives is union with God, the elements of the liturgy are real spiritual performances leading us to God: "Through

60 Ibid.
61 Ibid., 24
62 Ibid.

the holy partaking of the immaculate and life-giving mysteries, grace brings about the fellowship and identity with God according to participation that is possible through our likeness to God, and through this identity man is deemed worthy to become god from man."[63] Still, Maximus reserves finality for our experiences of grace for a time beyond this life: "We believe that we have partaken of the gifts of the Holy Spirit through grace by faith here in this present life, and we believe that . . . we shall partake in these things in their very reality—in the age to come according to that which is ultimately true. . . ."[64]

III. The Transmission of the *Ecclesiastical Mystagogy*:

There are 40 manuscripts that preserve either the complete or partial text of *On the Ecclesiastical Mystagogy*.[65] In the Corpus Christianorum Series Greca edition of the text, Christian Boudignon offers a concise description of each manuscript, including a material description and an estimated or exact dating.[66] The manuscripts range from the tenth to the eighteenth centuries, with five manuscripts dating to the tenth century. Information concerning the provenance of each manuscript and the library that formerly owned the manuscript is listed when known; occasionally the names of those involved in the copying or acquisition of the manuscript are provided. In the case of lacunae—and lacunae affect most of the manuscripts to some degree—the lines missing are noted. The infrequent marginal notes that appear throughout the manuscripts are noted and their contents described. Boudignon evaluates the testimony to the original text of *On the Ecclesiastical Mystagogy* from the passages reproduced in several medieval sources: the letter by Mark Eugenikos (15th century), the *Ecclesiastical History* by Germanus of Constantinople (8th

---

[63]Ibid.

[64]Ibid.

[65]Maximus the Confessor, *Mystagogia*, ed. Christian Boudignon, *Corpus Christianorum Series Graeca* (Turnhout: Brepols, 2011), xiii–xiv.

[66]Ibid., xiv–xlvii.

century), the catena on the Gospel of Luke by Nicetas of Heraclea (11th century), and various florilegia. Finally, Boudignon surveys the printed editions of the text, beginning with Gentien Hervet's Latin translation published in 1548 and concluding with Charalampos Sotiropoulos' edition of the Greek text that appeared in his 1978 doctoral dissertation at the University of Athens.[67]

The past century has witnessed a remarkable flowering of studies on Maximus the Confessor.[68] The modern rediscovery of Maximus began in 1869 with Hermann Weser's dissertation at the University of Halle.[69] For nearly seventy years, the scholarly literature tended to portray Maximus as a noncreative theologian, a voice merely reiterating the dogmatic definitions of Chalcedon. This began to change with Sergei Epifanovich's 1915 study, *Venerable Maximus the Confessor and Byzantine Theology*,[70] which portrayed Maximus in the context of the Byzantine culture of the seventh century, emphasizing the ascetic-mystical elements in Maximus' theology. The watershed moment, however, came in 1941, when Hans Urs von Balthasar—one of the luminaries of the *Ressourcement* movement and an associate of Henri de Lubac and Jean Daniélou—published the first edition of his monograph on Maximus under the title *Kosmische Liturgie: Höhe und Krise des griechischen Weltbildes bei Maximus Confessor*.[71] Before the second edition appeared in 1961, von Balthasar completed studies on Origen, Evagrius, Gregory of Nyssa, and Pseudo-Dionysius,

[67]Ibid., clx–clxxvii.

[68]See Joshua Lollar, "Reception of Maximian Thought in the Modern Era," in *The Oxford Handbook of Maximus the Confessor*, ed. Pauline Allen and Bronwen Neil (Oxford: University Press, 2015), 564–580; Andrew Louth, "Recent Research on St Maximus the Confessor: A Survey," *St Vladimir's Theological Quarterly* 42 (1998): 67–84; Thunberg, *Microcosm and Mediator*, 12–20; Blowers, "Recontextualizations of Maximus East and West," in *Maximus the Confessor: Jesus Christ and the Transfiguration of the World*, 287–328.

[69]*S. Maximi Confessoris praecepta de incarnatione dei et deificatione hominis exponuntur et examinantur: dissertatio historico-dogmatica* (Berlin: Windolf, 1869).

[70]*Prepodobniy Maksim Ispovednik i vizantiskoe bogoslovie* (Kiev: Barskii, 1915).

[71]The second edition of which has been translated into English by Brian Daley, S.J., as *Cosmic Liturgy: The Universe according to Maximus the Confessor* (San Francisco: Ignatius, 2003).

and this second edition of von Balthasar's oeuvre has immensely influenced the reception of Maximus' theology since. In the years following von Balthasar's publication, scholars began to acquire new respect for Maximus' method of constructing dogmatic theology from the diverse streams of Christian tradition and forging them into a unified synthesis.[72] Landmark studies on Maximus' writings and theology by Polycarp Sherwood, Walther Völker, Lars Thunberg, Paul M. Blowers, and Andrew Louth followed in the second half of the twentieth century. In the twenty-first century, scholarly interest has become so keen and scholarly research so prolific that bibliographies have been published and international congresses orchestrated dedicated solely to Maximus the Confessor.

---

[72]In Lollar's review of the research: "He [Maximus] was for von Balthasar, as he was for Epifanovich, an 'heir' of the tradition, not simply a compiler. Heirs receive the property of their forebears as their own and increase it if they know how. This Maximus certainly did know, and he stands not as a passive recipient but as a theological artist who, working with the traditional materials available to us all, created something reflective of his own unique vision" ("Reception of Maximian Thought in the Modern Era," 569).

ΜΥΣΤΑΓΩΓΙΑ[1]

Περὶ τοῦ τίνων σύμβολα τὰ κατὰ
τὴν ἁγίαν Ἐκκλησίαν ἐπὶ τῆς[2] συνάξεως
τελούμενα καθεστήκη.[3]

ΠΡΟΟΙΜΙΟΝ[4]

<657c> Πῶς σοφώτερος γίνεται λαβὼν ἀφορμὴν ὁ σοφός, καὶ
δίκαιος γνοὺς προσθήσει τοῦ δέχεσθαι, κατὰ τὴν θείαν παροιμίαν,
σαφῶς αὐτός, πάντων μοι τιμιώτατε, κατ' αὐτὴν ἔδειξας τὴν
πεῖραν, ἔργῳ διδάξας ὅπερ ὁ θεῖος σοφῶς ὑπαινίσσεται λόγος.
ἅπαξ γὰρ ἀκούσας μου κατ' ἐπιδρομὴν ἐπιτόμως, ὡς οἷόν τε ἦν,
ἀφηγουμένου τὰ ἄλλῳ τινὶ μεγάλῳ γέροντι, καὶ ὄντως τὰ θεῖα
σοφῷ περί τε τῆς ἁγίας Ἐκκλησίας, καὶ τῆς ἐν αὐτῇ ἐπιτελουμένης
ἁγίας συνάξεως. καλῶς τε καὶ μυστικῶς θεωρηθέντα, καὶ ὡς ἐνῆν
μάλιστα διδασκαλικῶς, ἀπήτεις με κατεπείγων <660a> ἐξαυτῆς,
ἔγγραφόν σοι ποιεῖσθαι τὴν τούτων διήγησιν, λήθης φάρμακον
καὶ βοήθειαν μνήμης ἔχειν τὸ γράμμα βεβουλημένος, φυσικῶς τὸν
χρόνον ἐχούσης φάσκων δαμάζοντα· καὶ ἀνεπαισθήτως διὰ λήθης
τῶν ἐναποκειμένων καλῶν συλᾶν τε καὶ ἀφανίζειν παντελῶς τοὺς
τύπους καὶ τὰς εἰκόνας δυνάμενον, καὶ διὰ τοῦτο πάντως δεομένης
τοῦ ἀνακαινίζοντος τρόπου, καθ' ὃν ἡ τοῦ λόγου δύναμις διὰ
παντὸς ἀκμάζουσα συντηρεῖν πέφυκε τὴν μνήμην ἀπαθῆ καὶ

---

[1]Περί ἐκκλησιαστικῆς μυσταγωγίας CCSG
[2]τῆς θείας CCSG
[3]καθέστηκεν. Κυρίῳ θεοχαρίστῳ, Μάξιμος ταπεινὸς μοναχός CCSG
[4]om. CCSG

On the Ecclesiastical Mystagogy

On the Symbolism that Has Been Established for the Rites that are Performed by the Holy Church at the Divine Synaxis.

To Lord Theocharistos,[1] Maximus the humble monk:

The divine proverb says, "a wise man" becomes "wiser" when he receives "an opportunity," and "a righteous man" when he knows [5] "will continue to receive knowledge,"[2] and, by your experience, most honorable of all to me, you clearly showed this to be true, teaching by action what the divine word wisely intimates. You once listened to me relating in a cursory and summary fashion—such as [CCSG 4] it was—the contemplations of another esteemed elder, who is truly [10] wise in divine things concerning both the holy Church and the divine synaxis that is performed in her. Since the contemplations were beautiful and mystical and, above all, valuable for teaching, you pleaded with me to draft for you a written exposition of these rites from the synaxis. You wished to have this book as a "remedy against forgetfulness"[3] and an aid to memory, saying that time naturally [15] overpowers the memory and can imperceptibly through forgetfulness strip away and even completely obliterate the impressions and images of the beautiful things that are stored in the memory. For this reason, memory doubtless stands in need of a way[4] of renewal

[1] Theocharistos is a name that means "God is gracious," "favored by God," or "pleasing to God."

[2] Prov 9.9.

[3] Clement of Alexandria, *Stromata* 1.1.

[4] This is the first of several notable instances in which Maximus places λόγος and τρόπος in juxtaposition.

ἀμείωτον. ὅσον δὲ τοῦ ἁπλῶς ἀκούειν τὸ καὶ διαμονὴν ἀκαθαίρετον τῶν ἀκουσθέντων ἐπιζητεῖν ἐστι σοφώτερον, ἐπίσταται πάντως πᾶς ὁ καὶ μικρὸν εὐγενείας λογικῆς ἐπιμελούμενος, καὶ μὴ πάντη τῆς πρὸς τὸν λόγον οἰκειότητος ὑπάρχων ἀλλότριος.

<660b> Κἀγὼ μὲν ὤκνουν παρὰ τὴν ἀρχήν, τοῦ λόγου[5]— εἰρήσεται γὰρ τἀληθές—τὴν ὑπόθεσιν παραιτούμενος· οὐ τῷ μὴ θέλειν ὑμῖν, ἠγαπημένοι, παντὶ τρόπῳ διδόναι κατὰ δύναμιν τὸ καταθύμιον, ἀλλὰ τῷ μήτε τῆς ἐναγούσης πρὸς τοῦτο τοὺς ἀξίους μετειληφέναι χάριτος, μήτε τὴν πεῖραν ἔχειν τῆς πρὸς τὸ λέγειν δυνάμεώς τε καὶ τριβῆς, ἰδιωτείᾳ συντεθραμμένος καὶ λόγων τεχνικῶν παντελῶς ἀμύητος ὑπάρχων τῶν ἐν μόνῃ τῇ προσφορᾷ τὴν χάριν ἐχόντων, οἷς οἱ πολλοὶ μάλιστα χαίρουσι τῇ ἀκοῇ τὴν ἡδονὴν περιγράφοντες, κἂν εἰ μηδὲν τῶν τιμίων διὰ βάθους πολλάκις ἔχοιεν· καὶ τῷ, [ὡς][6] κυριώτερον εἰπεῖν καὶ ἀληθέστερον, δεδοικέναι μὴ καθυβρίσειν, τῇ εὐτελείᾳ τοῦ ἡμετέρου λόγου, τὴν ἐκείνου τοῦ μακαρίου ἀνδρὸς περὶ τῶν θείων ὑψηγορίαν τε καὶ νόησιν.

<660c> Ὅμως δ᾽ οὖν ὕστερον τῇ βίᾳ τῆς ἀγάπης εἴξας τῆς πάντων ἰσχυροτέρας ἐδεξάμην ἑκὼν τὸ ἐπίταγμα, γελᾶσθαι μᾶλλον ἐπ᾽ αὐθαδείᾳ τε καὶ ἀπαιδευσίᾳ δι᾽ εὐπείθειαν παρὰ τῶν μεμψιμοίρων ἑλόμενος ἢ ὑμῖν διὰ τῆς ἀναβολῆς ἐν παντὶ καλῷ μὴ συμπροθυμεῖσθαι βούλεσθαι νομισθῆναι, τὴν περὶ τοῦ πῶς εἰπεῖν μέριμναν τῷ Θεῷ ἐπιρρίψας τῷ μόνῳ θαυματουργῷ καὶ διδάσκοντι μὲν ἄνθρωπον γνῶσιν, τρανοῦντι δὲ γλῶσσαν μογιλάλων, καὶ τοῖς

---

[5]τοῦ λόγου : τὸν λόγον CCSG
[6]om. CCSG

by which the power of the written word continually abounds and by nature preserves the memory unchanged and undiminished. Everyone who is endowed with a little of the nobility of reason and is not completely estranged from intimacy with the word surely knows how much wiser it is to seek the indestructible permanence of that which is heard than simply to hear.   [20]

But at first "the reason I was reluctant, for—I will speak the truth"[5]—I declined your proposal, beloved readers, was not because I did not wish to give you my thoughts in any way to the best of my [25] ability, but because I have not partaken of the grace that leads those who are worthy into such an undertaking. Neither do I have experi- [30] ence in the art and practice of speaking, since I was educated rudely and am completely uninitiated in the craft of words—which possess merit in the delivery alone, in which the masses greatly delight, lim- iting their pleasure to the sound of the words, even if the words often contain nothing of the value of deep insight. But it would be nobler[6] [35] and truer to say that I was anxious lest, by the economy of our dis- course, I should insult the majestic expression and intelligence of that blessed man concerning divine things.

Nevertheless, at last yielding to the compulsion of love, which [40] is stronger than all, I accepted your demand willingly. For, I would rather be laughed at by the critics for audacity and lack of education while being obedient than let it be supposed by my postponement that I do not wish to share in your eagerness for every good thing. As it says, "cast" your "anxieties"[7] on God, the only one who works wonders and "teaches man knowledge,"[8] who makes intelligible the [45] "tongue of stammerers,"[9] who finds a way "for those who are lost,"[10]

---

[5]Gregory of Nazianzus, *Oration* 43.2.

[6]κυριώτερον; this comparative adjective from the noun κύριος literally means "more lordly." In certain patristic contexts, this term and related terms can refer to the Christological reading of Scripture—i.e., the reading pertaining to the Lord.

[7]1 Pet 5.7.
[8]Ps 93.10.
[9]Is 35.6.
[10]Gregory of Nazianzus, *Oration* 42.5.

ἀπόροις πόρον ἐπινοοῦντι καὶ ἐγείροντι μὲν ἀπὸ γῆς πτωχόν, ἀπὸ
δὲ κοπρίας ἀνυψοῦντι πένητα· τοῦ σαρκικοῦ λέγω φρονήματος
καὶ τῆς δυσώδους τῶν παθῶν ἰλύος· τὸν πτωχὸν τῷ πνεύματι ἢ
τὸν κακίας πτωχεύοντα, καὶ τῆς κατ᾽ αὐτὴν πενόμενον ἕξεως,
ἢ τοὐναντίον καὶ τὸν ἔτι τῷ νόμῳ <660d> τῆς σαρκὸς καὶ τοῖς
πάθεσιν ἐνεχόμενον καὶ διὰ τοῦτο τῆς κατ᾽ ἀρετὴν καὶ γνῶσιν
πτωχεύοντα καὶ πενόμενον χάριτος.

Ἀλλ᾽ ἐπειδὴ τῷ παναγίῳ καὶ ὄντως θεοφάντορι Διονυσίῳ τῷ
Ἀρεοπαγίτῃ ἐν τῇ Περὶ τῆς ἐκκλησιαστικῆς ἱεραρχίας πραγματείᾳ
καὶ τὰ κατὰ τὴν ἱερὰν <661a> τῆς ἁγίας συνάξεως τελετὴν ἀξίως τῆς
αὐτοῦ μεγαλονοίας τεθεώρηται σύμβολα, ἰστέον ὡς οὐ τὰ αὐτὰ
νῦν ὁ λόγος διεξέρχεται, οὔτε διὰ τῶν αὐτῶν ἐκείνῳ προέρχεται.
τολμηρὸν γὰρ καὶ αὔθαδες καὶ ἀπονοίας ἐγγύς, ἐγχειρεῖν τοῖς
ἐκείνου πειρᾶσθαι τὸν[7] μήτε χωρεῖν αὐτὸν ἢ νοεῖν δυνάμενον,[8]
καὶ ὡς ἴδια προκομίζειν τὰ ἐνθέως ἐκείνῳ μόνῳ διὰ τοῦ Πνεύματος
φανερωθέντα μυστήρια, ἀλλ᾽ ὅσα καὶ ἄλλοις ὡς ληπτὰ παρ᾽
αὐτοῦ φιλανθρώπως βουλήσει Θεοῦ παρελείφθη πρὸς ἔκθεσιν καὶ
γυμνασίαν τῆς αὐτῶν ἐκείνων περὶ τὰ θεῖα κατὰ τὴν ἔφεσιν ἕξεως,
καὶ δι᾽ ὧν συμμέτρως αὐτοῖς ἡ παμφαὴς τῶν τελουμένων ἀκτὶς
κατανοουμένη καθίσταται γνώριμος καὶ πρὸς ἑαυτὴν κατέχει τῷ

[7] τοὺς CCSG
[8] δυνάμενον : δυναμένους CCSG

who "raises the poor one from the ground" and "lifts" the "needy one
from" the "trash heap"[11]—I am speaking of the fleshly thoughts and [CCSG 6]
malodorous slime of the passions. And the poor one is the "poor in
spirit"[12] or the one who is impoverished concerning evil and desti- [50]
tute of the habit according to it, or contrariwise, the poor one is the
one who is still entangled in the law of the flesh and in the passions
and, for this reason, impoverished and destitute of the grace according to virtue and knowledge.

But since the symbols according to the sacred rite of the holy
synaxis have been contemplated by the all-holy and truly God-
revealing Dionysius the Areopagite, in a fashion worthy of his [55]
expansive mind, in his treatise, *On the Ecclesiastical Hierarchy*, one
should know that the present discourse does not cover the same
things, nor does it advance through the same things as his—for it
would be audacity and arrogance and near insanity for those who [60]
are not able to attain to or comprehend him to attempt to emulate
him and to present as their own the mysteries that were revealed by
the inspiration through the Spirit to that one alone—but [the present
discourse covers] as many things as are attainable[13] to others and
as in the benevolent will of God he omitted for the displaying and [CCSG 7]
training of their habit concerning divine things according to their [65]
desire.[14] When perceived through the divine things, the "radiant

[11] Ps 112.7.

[12] τὸν πτωχὸν τῷ πνεύματι; Maximus' citation is in the singular ("the poor one")
whereas Matthew 5.3 is in the plural ("those who are poor").

[13] ληπτός ("perceptible," specifically by the senses); the word comes to be used as
the opposite of νοητός ("intelligible").

[14] Here one can clearly see Pseudo-Dionysius' influence on Maximus. Pseudo-
Dionysius had written: "Now it may be that some explanation is due for the fact that
even though Hierotheus, our famous teacher, has put together his splendid *Elements
of Theology*, I too have composed other theological works together with this present
one as though what he wrote were not quite sufficient. If he had set out to deal with all
theological questions and indeed had provided an account of every area of theology,
I would not have been so mad or foolish as to believe that in dealing with these same
theological topics I could have displayed a more divine insight than he, and certainly
I would not have wasted time in a repetition of these same things" (*On the Divine
Names* 3.2 [trans. Luibheid, p. 69]).

πόθῳ περιληφθέντας, ἵνα μὴ παντελῶς οἱ μετ' αὐτὸν ὦσιν ἀργοί, τὴν πᾶσαν τοῦ <661b> χρόνου τῆς παρούσης ζωῆς ἡμέραν, οὐκ ἔχοντες τὸν πρὸς τὴν θείαν ἐκείνην ἀμπελουργίαν μισθούμενον λόγον, τὸν ὑπὲρ τῆς πνευματικῆς ἐργασίας τοῦ πνευματικοῦ ἀμπελῶνος, τὸ συλωθὲν κατ' ἀρχὰς ὑπὸ τοῦ πονηροῦ δι' ἀπάτης κατὰ τὴν τῆς ἐντολῆς παράβασιν, πνευματικὸν τῆς θείας καὶ βασιλικωτάτης εἰκόνος δηνάριον ἀποδιδόντα.

Οὐ πάντα δὲ τὰ τῷ μακαρίῳ γέροντι μυστικῶς θεωρηθέντα λέγειν καθεξῆς ἐπαγγέλλομαι· οὐδ' αὐτὰ τὰ λεγόμενα, ὡς ἐνοήθη τε παρ' ἐκείνου καὶ ἐλέχθη. ἐκεῖνος γάρ, πρὸς τὸ φιλόσοφος εἶναι καὶ πάσης <661c> παιδείας διδάσκαλος, δι' ἀρετῆς περιουσίαν καὶ τῆς περὶ τὰ θεῖα χρονιωτέρας τε καὶ ἐπιστημονικωτέρας τριβῆς καὶ φιλοπονίας, τῶν τῆς ὕλης δεσμῶν καὶ τῶν κατ' αὐτὴν φαντασιῶν ἐλεύθερον ἑαυτὸν καταστήσας, τόν τε νοῦν εἰκότως εἶχε ταῖς θείαις αὐγαῖς περιλαμπόμενον, καὶ διὰ τοῦτο δυνάμενον εὐθέως ὁρᾶν τὰ τοῖς πολλοῖς μὴ ὁρώμενα, καὶ τὸν λόγον ἑρμηνευτὴν ἀκριβέστατον τῶν νοηθέντων· καὶ ἐσόπτρου δίκην ὑπ' οὐδεμιᾶς κηλίδος παθῶν ἐμποδιζόμενον, ἀκραιφνῶς τὰ ἄλλοις μήτε νοηθῆναι δυνάμενα, καὶ φέρειν καὶ λέγειν ἰσχύοντα, ὡς δύνασθαι τοὺς ἀκροατὰς ὅλον μὲν τῷ λόγῳ τὸν νοῦν ὁρᾶν ἐποχούμενον· ὅλα δὲ ὅλῳ τῷ νῷ καθαρῶς ἐμφαίνεσθαι τὰ νοηθέντα καὶ διὰ τῆς τοῦ λόγου μεσιτείας αὐτοῖς διαπορθμευόμενα δέξασθαι· ἀλλ'

splendor"[15] of the rites performed is made manifest to them in due measure, and it binds to itself those who are encompassed by longing "in order that" those who come after the blessed elder "should not be altogether idle"[16] all the day of the time of the present life because they do not have a paid contract to work in the divine vineyard. [70] This contract for spiritual work in the spiritual vineyard restores[17] the spiritual denarius of the divine and most royal image[18] that was stolen by the evil one in the beginning through deceit according to the transgression of the commandment.

Now, I am not promising to recount all that which was contem- [75] plated mystically by the blessed elder, nor the same things that he said, as he perceived and said them. (For in order to become a lover of wisdom and a teacher of every discipline, he set himself free from the fetters of matter and its delusions by a superabundance of virtue and [80; by the study of the divine things for a long time and in an expert fash- CCSG 8] ion and by hard work. And consequently his mind was illuminated by the divine light, and so he was able to see by inspiration things that are invisible to the masses. And his discourse, like a mirror, undimin- ished by any stain of the passions, is a most accurate interpreter of that which he perceived, receiving in an untainted fashion the things [85] that others were not able to perceive. And the discourse succeeds in conveying and saying things so that his hearers are able to see the whole thought communicated in the discourse and that all the things that he perceived are reflected purely in the whole thought and fer- ried across through the mediation of the discourse.)[19] But whatever [90]

---

[15]Pseudo-Dionysius, *Epistle* 10. The addressee of this epistle is John the Apostle, as though still exiled on Patmos. For Pseudo-Dionysius, the mystical tradition finds one of its major streams in the teachings of John the Apostle.

[16]Gregory of Nazianzus, Oration 45.12 (trans. Harrison, p. 171); cf. Mt 20.6.

[17]ἀποδίδωμι can also be a financial term meaning "to pay back."

[18]For Maximus, the "spiritual denarius" represents the *imago Dei*; as a denarius bears the image of the king whose authority gives the denarius its value, so man reflects the image of his Creator.

[19]διὰ τῆς τοῦ λόγου μεσιτείας; in this instance, Maximus probably intends the reader to understand λόγος not only as the present discourse but also as the divine λόγος, the reason by which everything is intelligible.

ὅσα διὰ μνήμης τε φέρω, καὶ ὡς <661d> νοεῖν ἀμυδρῶς καὶ λέγειν ἀμυδρότερον δύναμαι, πλὴν εὐσεβῶς χάριτι τοῦ τὰ ἐσκοτισμένα φωτίζοντος Θεοῦ. μηδὲ γὰρ οἴεσθαι δεῖν ὑμᾶς ὑπολαμβάνω, δικαίως κρίνειν εἰδότας, ἄλλως με νοεῖν ἢ λέγειν δύνασθαι ἢ ὡς νοεῖν καὶ λέγειν δύναμαι καὶ ἡ ἄνωθεν χάρις ἐνδίδωσιν, οἰκείως τῆς ἀναλογούσης μοι προνοουμένης δυνάμεως, κἂν ὁ παραδοὺς μάλιστα καὶ διδάξας ἐστὶν ὑψηλότατος. ἐπεὶ τὸ τὰ ἴσα ζητεῖν παρὰ τῶν μὴ ἴσων τὴν ἀρετὴν καὶ τὴν γνῶσιν οὐ πόρρω μοι δοκεῖ τυγχάνειν τῶν δεῖξιν πειρωμένων τῷ ἡλίῳ κατὰ τὸ ἴσον τὴν σελήνην <664a> φωτίζουσαν· καὶ τὰ μὴ πάντη ταῦτα συμβαίνειν ἀλλήλοις κατὰ πάντα δύνασθαι βιαζομένων, ὅπερ ἀμήχανον καὶ ἀδύνατον.[9]

Ἡγείσθω δὲ Θεὸς τῶν λεγομένων τε καὶ νοουμένων, ὁ μόνος νοῦς τῶν νοούντων καὶ νοουμένων, καὶ λόγος τῶν λεγόντων καὶ λεγομένων, καὶ ζωὴ τῶν ζώντων καὶ ζωουμένων, καὶ πᾶσι πάντα καὶ ὢν καὶ γινόμενος, δι᾽ αὐτὰ τὰ ὄντα καὶ γινόμενα· δι᾽ ἑαυτὸν δὲ οὐδὲν κατ᾽ οὐδένα τρόπον οὐδαμῶς οὔτε ὢν οὔτε γινόμενος, τῶν ἅ τι τῶν ὄντων ἐστὶ καὶ <664b> γινομένων, οἷα μηδενὶ τὸ παράπαν τῶν ὄντων φυσικῶς συντασσόμενος, καὶ διὰ τοῦτο τὸ μὴ εἶναι μᾶλλον, διὰ τὸ ὑπερεῖναι, ὡς οἰκειότερον ἐπ᾽ αὐτοῦ λεγόμενον προσιέμενος. δεῖ γάρ, εἴπερ ὡς ἀληθῶς τὸ γνῶναι διαφορὰν Θεοῦ καὶ κτισμάτων ἐστὶν ἀναγκαῖον ἡμῖν, θέσιν εἶναι τοῦ ὑπερόντος τὴν τῶν ὄντων ἀφαίρεσιν, καὶ τὴν τῶν ὄντων θέσιν εἶναι τοῦ ὑπερόντος ἀφαίρεσιν, καὶ ἄμφω περὶ τὸν αὐτὸν κυρίως[10] θεωρεῖσθαι τὰς προσηγορίας, καὶ μηδεμίαν κυρίως δύνασθαι· τὸ εἶναι, φημί, καὶ μὴ εἶναι. ἄμφω μὲν κυρίως, ὡς τῆς μὲν τοῦ εἶναι

---

[9]καὶ ἀδύνατον om. CCSG
[10]κυρίως : εὐσεβῶς CCSG

I hold in my memory and am able to perceive dimly and to speak even more dimly, nevertheless with reverence, yet I will speak by the grace of the God who illuminates the things that have been darkened. I do not suppose that you, who know how to discern rightly, think it necessary for me to be able to perceive or to speak otherwise than as I am able to perceive and speak and as the grace from above grants. [95] This grace provides an ability that is properly accorded to me, even if the one who imparts and teaches you is ultimately the Most High, since it seems to me that to seek equal things from things that are unequal in virtue and knowledge would not be far from those who attempt to prove that the moon shines equally to the sun or those who force things that do not correspond to one another in any way [100] to correspond in every way, although this is preposterous.

Let God be the guide of the things that are perceived and spoken, [CCSG 9] for he is the only mind of those who perceive and of that which is perceived, and he is the only word of those who speak and of that [105] which is spoken. He is the life of the living and of the things that have been endowed with life. On account of the very things that are and that are becoming, he is the one who is and the one who "becomes all things to all."[20] But, on account of himself, he neither in any way whatsoever belongs to nor comes to belong to the things that are or that are becoming, whose essence he constitutes. He is by nature in the same class as absolutely nothing of the things that are, and for [110] this reason, he allows us to say rather that he is not, because it is more properly said of him that he transcends being.[21] For it is necessary, if we are to know truly the difference between God and creatures, we must know that the negation of the things that are is the affirmation of the one who transcends being, and the affirmation of the things that are is the negation of the one who transcends being. And both [115] designations can be reverently contemplated about him, yet neither

[20] 1 Cor 9.22.
[21] The idea of God being "beyond being" is not a foreign concept to neo-Platonic philosophy. Plotinus can write about the One (which some surmise corresponds to the first person of the Trinity in Christian theology) as the "One beyond being" [τὸ ἐπέκεινα ὄντος τὸ ἕν] (see *Enneads*, 5.1.10 [Armstrong, 5:45]).

τοῦ Θεοῦ κατ᾽ αἰτίαν τῶν ὄντων θετικῆς, τῆς δὲ καθ᾽ ὑπεροχὴν αἰτίας τοῦ εἶναι πάσης τῶν ὄντων ἀφαιρετικῆς· καὶ μηδὲ μίαν κυρίως πάλιν, ὡς οὐδεμιᾶς τὴν κατ᾽ <664c> οὐσίαν αὐτὴν καὶ φύσιν τοῦ τί εἶναι τοῦ ζητουμένου θέσιν παριστώσης. ᾧ γὰρ μηδὲν τὸ σύνολον φυσικῶς κατ᾽ αἰτίαν συνέζευκται, ἢ ὂν ἢ μὴ ὄν, τούτῳ οὐδὲν τῶν ὄντων καὶ λεγομένων, οὐδὲ τῶν μὴ ὄντων καὶ μὴ λεγομένων, εἰκότως ἐστὶν ἐγγύς. ἁπλῆν γὰρ καὶ ἄγνωστον καὶ πᾶσιν ἄβατον ἔχει τὴν ὕπαρξιν καὶ παντελῶς ἀνερμήνευτον, καὶ πάσης καταφάσεώς τε καὶ ἀποφάσεως οὖσαν ἐπέκεινα.

Καὶ ταῦτα μὲν περὶ τούτων· ἐπὶ δὲ τὴν προκειμένην τοῦ λόγου[11] ὑπόθεσιν ἔλθωμεν.

<664d> Κεφαλ.[12] Α. Πῶς τε καὶ ποίῳ τρόπῳ εἰκών ἐστι καὶ τύπος Θεοῦ ἡ ἁγία Ἐκκλησία

Τὴν τοίνυν ἁγίαν Ἐκκλησίαν, κατὰ πρώτην θεωρίας ἐπιβολήν, τύπον καὶ εἰκόνα Θεοῦ φέρειν ἔλεγεν ὁ μακάριος γέρων ἐκεῖνος, ὡς τὴν αὐτὴν αὐτῷ κατὰ μίμησιν καὶ τύπον ἐνέργειαν ἔχουσαν.

Ὥσπερ γὰρ ὁ Θεὸς πάντα τῇ ἀπείρῳ δυνάμει ποιήσας καὶ εἰς τὸ εἶναι παραγαγὼν συνέχει καὶ συνάγει καὶ περιγράφει, καὶ ἀλλήλοις καὶ ἑαυτῷ προνοητικῶς ἐνδιασφίγγει τά τε νοητὰ καὶ τὰ αἰσθητά, καὶ περὶ ἑαυτὸν ὡς αἰτίαν καὶ ἀρχὴν καὶ τέλος πάντα περικρατῶν τὰ κατὰ τὴν φύσιν ἀλλήλων διεστηκότα, κατὰ μίαν τὴν πρὸς αὐτὸν ὡς ἀρχὴν σχέσεως δύναμιν ἀλλήλοις συννενευκότα ποιεῖ, καθ᾽ ἣν

---

[11]τοῦ λόγου : τῷ λόγῳ CCSG
[12]Κεφαλ. om. everywhere CCSG, it will not be further noted.

is possible in a proper sense—I am speaking of the existence and non-existence of God. Both are possible in a proper sense: on the one hand, it can be affirmed that God is because he is the cause of the things that are, and, on the other hand, it can be completely negated that God is because of his superiority as cause of the things that are. And, again, neither is possible in a proper sense, because neither establishes the very essence and nature of what existence is concerning the one whom we seek. For nothing at all—whether it exists or does not exist—is united with him by nature because he is their cause; neither anything of the things that are and are spoken nor anything of the things that are not and are not spoken in any way comes near to him. For he has an existence that is simple and unknowable and inaccessible to everyone and that is completely indescribable and beyond every kataphatic and apophatic statement. [120; CCSG] [125]

This suffices for now. Let us proceed to the subject set before us in the discourse.

(1) How and in What Mode the Holy Church Is the Image and Representation of God

Therefore, as the first point of his contemplation, the blessed elder said that the holy Church bears the representation and image of God because she possesses the same activity as his according to imitation and representation. [230]

For as God made all things by his infinite power and brought them into existence, so now he sustains them and draws them together and defines their limits, and he providentially binds the intelligible and the sensible things to one another and to himself. And, because he possesses full command of everything around him as their cause, beginning, and end, he makes the things that have been set apart from one another by nature to be the things that have converged with one another by the one power of their relationship with him as their beginning. And it is by this power that all things are led to an identity of movement and existence that is indistinguishable [135; CCSG]

εἰς <665a> ταυτότητα κινήσεώς τε καὶ ὑπάρξεως ἀδιάφθορον καὶ
ἀσύγχυτον ἄγετει[13] τὰ πάντα πρὸς οὐδὲν οὐδενὸς τῶν ὄντων
προηγουμένως κατὰ φύσεως διαφορὰν ἢ κινήσεως στασιάζοντός
τε καὶ διαιρουμένου, πάντων πᾶσι κατὰ τὴν μίαν τῆς μόνης
ἀρχῆς καὶ αἰτίας ἀδιάλυτον σχέσιν τε καὶ φρουρὰν ἀφύρτως
συμπεφυκότων, τὴν πάσας τε καὶ ἐπὶ πᾶσι κατὰ τὴν ἑκάστου τῶν
ὄντων φύσιν θεωρουμένας ἰδικὰς σχέσεις καταργοῦσάν τε καὶ
ἐπικαλύπτουσαν, οὐ τῷ φθείρειν αὐτὰς καὶ ἀναιρεῖν[14] καὶ μὴ εἶναι
ποιεῖν, ἀλλὰ τῷ νικᾶν καὶ ὑπερφαίνεσθαι, ὥσπερ ὁλότης μερῶν ἢ
καὶ αὐτῆς αἰτία τῆς ὁλότητος ἐπιφαινομένη, καθ᾽ ἣν ἥ τε ὁλότης
αὐτὴ καὶ τὰ τῆς ὁλότητος μέρη φαίνεσθαί τε καὶ εἶναι πέφυκεν,
ὡς ὅλην ἔχοντα τὴν αἰτίαν ἑαυτῶν ὑπερλάμπουσαν, καὶ ὥσπερ
ἥλιος <665b> ὑπερφανεὶς ἀστέρων καὶ φύσιν καὶ δύναμιν, οὕτω τὴν
αὐτῶν ὡς αἰτιατῶν αἰτίαν καλύπτουσαν ὕπαρξιν.

Πέφυκε γὰρ ὥσπερ ἐκ τῆς ὁλότητος τὰ μέρη, οὕτω δὲ[15] κἀκ
τῆς αἰτίας τὰ αἰτιατὰ καὶ εἶναι κυρίως καὶ γνωρίζεσθαι, καὶ τὴν

---

[13] ἄγεται CCSG
[14] ἀνελεῖν CCSG
[15] δὴ CCSG

and without confusion;[22] all things are led to absolutely nothing that is originally and according to a difference of nature and motion discordant and divided from the things that are.[23] All things have been united with all things without confusion[24] according to the one, irreducible[25] relationship and protection[26] of the only beginning and cause. This relationship nullifies and covers over all individual relationships that are contemplated according to the nature of each   [145] of the things that are, not because it corrupts and destroys them and causes them not to be, but because it surpasses and outshines them, just as the totality comes into view[27] rather than its parts and the cause of the totality itself comes into view rather than the totality. And it is by this relationship that the totality itself and the parts of the totality shine and by nature are, because the parts possess the whole   [150] cause, which shines more brilliantly than themselves. And just as the sun is more brilliant than the stars in nature and power, so also its appearance[28] covers over them as a cause does its effects.

For just as by nature the parts are from the totality, so also the effects are properly and are made known from the cause, and the   [155]

---

[22]ἀσύγχυτος; this Greek term appears in the Chalcedonian definition as one of the "four fences" and is translated "without confusion."

[23]Maximus is saying that it is by the power of the relationship of all things with God that they are reconciled to God and to one another. Therefore all things are oriented to God in their original, created form, and it is by relationship with God that all things achieve unity with one another; nothing in its original, created form is oriented to the division and discord that comes as a result of the fracturing of relationship with God.

[24]ἀφύρτως; this term is not one of the "four fences" of Chalcedon.

[25]ἀδιάλυτος; the term means "indissoluble," but here the sense must be that all relationships cannot be reduced beyond the relationship with God; all things find their unity in the commonality of their relationship to God.

[26]φρουρά; Maximus is saying that because all things have a relationship with God as their beginning and cause, God also then has a protective, providential role toward all of creation.

[27]ἐπιφαίνω; the sense in the passive is "to come into view," "to present oneself," "to appear upon the surface." Thus, Maximus' point is that when one views an entity, one sees the totality of this entity, not its composite parts. And, ultimately, when one reflects on any entity, one will be drawn back to reflect on the cause of this entity, which is God.

[28]ὕπαρξις; elsewhere, this term is also translated "existence."

ἑαυτῶν σχολάζουσαν ἔχειν ἰδιότητα, ἡνίκα τῆς πρὸς τὴν αἰτίαν ἀναφορᾶς[16] περιληφθέντα ποιωθῇ δι' ὅλου, κατὰ τὴν μίαν, ὡς εἴρεται, τῆς πρὸς αὐτὴν σχέσεως δύναμιν. πάντα γὰρ ἐν πᾶσιν ὤν, ὁ ἀπείροις μέτροις ὑπὲρ πάντα Θεός, μονώτατος τοῖς καθαροῖς τὴν διάνοιαν ὁραθήσεται· ἡνίκα ὁ νοῦς τοὺς τῶν ὄντων θεωρητικῶς ἀναλεγόμενος λόγους εἰς αὐτὸν καταλήξει τὸν Θεόν, ὡς αἰτίαν καὶ ἀρχὴν καὶ τέλος τῆς τῶν ὅλων παραγωγῆς καὶ γενέσεως καὶ πυθμένα τῆς πάντων περιοχῆς ἀδιάστατον.

<665c> Κατὰ τὸν αὐτὸν τρόπον καὶ ἡ ἁγία τοῦ Θεοῦ Ἐκκλησία τὰ αὐτὰ τῷ Θεῷ περὶ ἡμᾶς ὡς ἀρχετύπῳ εἰκὼν ἐνεργοῦσα δειχθήσεται. πολλῶν γὰρ ὄντων καὶ ἀπείρων ἀριθμῷ σχεδὸν ἀνδρῶν τε καὶ γυναικῶν καὶ παίδων, γένει καὶ εἴδει, καὶ ἔθνεσι καὶ γλώσσαις, καὶ βίοις καὶ ἡλικίαις, καὶ γνώμαις καὶ τέχναις, καὶ τρόποις καὶ ἤθεσι καὶ ἐπιτηδεύμασιν, ἐπιστήμαις τε αὖ καὶ ἀξιώμασι, καὶ τύχαις καὶ χαρακτῆρσι καὶ ἕξεσιν, ἀλλήλων διῃρημένων τε καὶ πλεῖστον διαφερόντων τῶν εἰς αὐτὴν γιγνομένων καὶ ὑπ' αὐτῆς ἀναγεννωμένων τε καὶ ἀναδημιουργουμένων τῷ Πνεύματι, μίαν πᾶσι κατὰ τὸ ἴσον δίδωσι καὶ χαρίζεται θείαν μορφὴν καὶ προσηγορίαν, τὸ ἀπὸ Χριστοῦ καὶ εἶναι καὶ ὀνομάζεσθαι· καὶ <665d>

[16] ἀναφορᾷ CCSG

cause holds the particularities of the effects at rest, and when the effects are comprehended by their reference to the cause, they are given quality wholly[29] according to the one power of their relation- [CCSG 12] ship to the cause, as I said above. For only God alone, who is "all things in all"[30] and who is by boundless measure above all, "will be seen by the pure" in their understanding.[31] When the mind perceives in contemplation the principles of the things that are, it [160] will end in God himself, as the cause and beginning and end of the creation and origin and as the everlasting foundation of the compass of the whole universe.

It will be shown that the holy Church of God works[32] the same things and in the same way as God does around us, as an image relates to its archetype. For, from among men, women, and chil- [165] dren, nearly boundless in number, who are many in race and class and nation and language and occupation and age and persuasion and trade and manners and customs and pursuits, and again, those who are divided and most different from one another in expertise [170] and worth and fortune and features and habits, those who are in the holy Church and are regenerated by her and are recreated by the Spirit[33]—to all he gives equally and grants freely one divine form and designation, that is to be and to be called from Christ. And he gives according to faith the one simple, indivisible,[34] and undivided

[29]It appears that Maximus writes "wholly" above in order to reinforce his point that when a part stands in relation to the whole, its quality is derived from the whole. Δι' ὅλου literally means "through the whole," but its sense is adverbial in this context.

[30]1 Cor 15.28.

[31]Mt 5.8.

[32]ἐνεργέω; see the very beginning of chapter 1, where Maximus says that the Church has the same "activity" [ἐνέργεια] as God.

[33]Maximus appeals to wordplay here. He places a pair of homophones (speaking of those who "are" [γινομένων] and those who "are regenerated" [ἀναγεννωμένων]) next to a word ("regenerated" [ἀναδημιουργουμένων]) that shares the suffix of the former and the prefix of the latter and that has the significant term for "work" [ἐνεργέω] embedded in its stem.

[34]ἀμερής: one can see from the composition of the word that it means "without parts." In light of the previous discourse concerning parts and the whole, it is clear

μίαν τὴν κατὰ πίστιν ἁπλῆν τε καὶ ἀμερῆ καὶ ἀδιαίρετον σχέσιν,
τὴν τὰς πολλὰς καὶ ἀμυθήτους περὶ ἕκαστον οὔσας διαφοράς,
οὐδ᾽ ὅτι κἂν εἰσὶ συγχωροῦσαν γνωρίζεσθαι, διὰ τὴν τῶν πάντων
εἰς αὐτὴν καθολικὴν ἀναφορὰν καὶ συνέλευσιν, καθ᾽ ἣν οὐδεὶς
τὸ παράπαν οὐδὲν ἑαυτῷ τοῦ κοινοῦ διωρισμένος ἐστί, πάντων
συμπεφυκότων ἀλλήλοις καὶ <668a> συνημμένων κατὰ τὴν μίαν
ἁπλῆν τε καὶ ἀδιαίρετον τῆς πίστεως χάριν καὶ δύναμιν. ἣν γὰρ
πάντων, φησίν, ἡ καρδία καὶ ἡ ψυχὴ μία· ὡς ἐκ διαφόρων μελῶν
σῶμα ἓν καὶ εἶναι καὶ ὁρᾶσθαι καὶ αὐτοῦ Χριστοῦ τῆς ἀληθινῆς
ἡμῶν κεφαλῆς ὄντως ἄξιον· ἐν ᾧ, φησὶν ὁ θεῖος πόστολος, οὐκ
ἔστιν ἄρρεν οὐδὲ θῆλυ, οὔτε Ἰουδαῖος οὔτε Ἕλλην, οὔτε περιτομὴ
οὔτε ἀκροβυστία, οὔτε βάρβαρος οὔτε Σκύθης, οὔτε δοῦλος οὔτε
ἐλεύθερος· ἀλλὰ πάντα καὶ ἐν πᾶσιν αὐτός, ὁ πάντα κατὰ μίαν
ἁπλῆν τῆς ἀγαθότητος ἀπειρόσοφον δύναμιν ἑαυτῷ περικλείων,
ὥσπερ κέντρον εὐθειῶν τινων ἐξημμένων αὐτοῦ, κατὰ μίαν ἁπλῆν
καὶ ἑνιαίαν αἰτίαν καὶ δύναμιν τὰς ἀρχὰς τῶν ὄντων τοῖς πέρασιν
οὐκ ἐῶν συναφίστασθαι, κύκλῳ περιγράφων <668b> αὐτῶν τὰς
ἐκτάσεις καὶ πρὸς ἑαυτὸν ἄγων τοὺς τῶν ὄντων καὶ ὑπ᾽ αὐτοῦ
γενομένων διορισμούς· ἵνα μὴ ἀλλήλων παντάπασιν ἀλλότρια ᾖ
καὶ ἐχθρὰ τὰ τοῦ ἑνὸς Θεοῦ κτίσματα καὶ ποιήματα, οὐκ ἔχοντα
περὶ τί καὶ ὅποι τὸ φίλον τι[17] καὶ εἰρηνικὸν καὶ ταυτὸν πρὸς
ἄλληλα δείξωσι, καὶ κινδυνεύσῃ αὐτοῖς καὶ αὐτὸ τὸ εἶναι εἰς τὸ μὴ
ὂν μεταπεσεῖν τοῦ Θεοῦ χωριζόμενον.

Εἰκὼν μὲν οὖν ἐστι τοῦ Θεοῦ, καθὼς εἴρηται, ἡ ἁγία Ἐκκλησία,
ὡς τὴν αὐτὴν τῷ Θεῷ περὶ τοὺς πιστοὺς ἐνεργοῦσα ἕνωσιν, κἂν
διάφοροι τοῖς ἰδιώμασι καὶ ἐκ διαφόρων καὶ τόπων καὶ τρόπων

---

[17] τι : τε CCSG

relationship, which does not allow the many and unspeakable differences about each one—even if they exist—to be known on account of the universal reference and union of all the people in the Church. According to this union, absolutely no one is separated by himself from the community because everyone has grown together and been joined to one another according to the one, simple, and undivided grace and power of the faith. For it says that "the heart and soul" of all "was one,"[35] as a body is composed of different members but is and is seen to be one; "and the body is actually worthy of Christ himself, who is our" true "head."[36] The divine apostle says that in Christ "there is neither male nor female, neither Jew nor Greek, neither circumcision nor uncircumcision, neither barbarian nor Scythian, neither slave nor free,"[37] but he is "all things and in all."[38] In his infinite wisdom, he encloses all things in himself according to the one, simple power of goodness, just as a center defines the lines that originate straight from it. According to the one, simple, and single cause and power, he does not permit the principles of the things that are to depart from their boundaries, but he limits their extents with a circle. And he leads the distinctions of the things that are and that are becoming by him to himself, in order that the things created and fashioned by the one God might not be altogether alien to and enemies of one another—since they have no reason and place to demonstrate amicability and peacefulness and identity toward one another—and that they might be safe from their very being changing into non-being, which is separation from God.

[175; CCSG 13]

[180]

[185]

[190]

[195; CCSG 14]

Therefore, the holy Church is the image of God, as it has been said, because she works the same oneness around the faithful as God does. And even if they are different in their characteristics, and from different places, and have different customs, those who are present

[200]

that Maximus is affirming that the relationship of all things with God reflects the fact that God is without parts.

[35] Acts 4.32.
[36] Gregory of Nazianzus, *Oration* 2.3.
[37] Gal 3.28.
[38] Col 3.11.

οἱ κατ᾽ αὐτὴν διὰ τῆς πίστεως ἐνοποιούμενοι τύχωσιν <668c> ὄντες, ἣν περὶ τὰς οὐσίας τῶν ὄντων ἀσυγχύτως αὐτὸς ἐνεργεῖν πέφυκεν ὁ Θεός, τὸ περὶ αὐτὰς διάφορον, ὡς δέδεικται, τῇ πρὸς ἑαυτὸν ὡς αἰτίαν καὶ ἀρχὴν καὶ τέλος ἀναφορᾷ τε καὶ ἑνώσει παραμυθούμενός τε καὶ ποιούμενος.

Κεφαλ. Β. Περὶ τοῦ πῶς καὶ τίνα τρόπον εἰκών ἐστι τοῦ ἐξ ὁρατῶν καὶ ἀοράτων οὐσιῶν ὑφεστῶτος[18] κόσμου ἡ ἁγία τοῦ Θεοῦ Ἐκκλησία

Κατὰ δευτέραν δὲ θεωρίας ἐπιβολήν, τοῦ σύμπαντος κόσμου τοῦ ἐξ ὁρατῶν καὶ ἀοράτων οὐσιῶν ὑφεστῶτος εἶναι τύπον καὶ εἰκόνα τὴν ἁγίαν τοῦ Θεοῦ Ἐκκλησίαν ἔφασκεν, ὡς τὴν αὐτὴν αὐτῷ καὶ ἕνωσιν καὶ διάκρισιν ἐπιδεχομένην.

Ὥσπερ γὰρ <668d> αὕτη κατὰ τὴν οἰκοδομὴν εἷς οἶκος ὑπάρχουσα τὴν κατὰ τὴν θέσιν τοῦ σχήματος ποιᾷ ἰδιότητι δέξεται[19] διαφοράν, διαιρουμένη εἴς τε τὸν μόνοις ἱερεῦσί τε καὶ λειτουργοῖς ἀπόκληρον τόπον, ὃν καλοῦμεν ἱερατεῖον, καὶ τὸν πᾶσι τοῖς πιστοῖς λαοῖς πρὸς ἐπίβασιν ἄνετον, ὃν καλοῦμεν ναόν—πάλιν μία ἐστὶ κατὰ τὴν ὑπόστασιν, οὐ συνδιαιρουμένη τοῖς ἑαυτῆς μέρεσι, διὰ τὴν ἑαυτῶν πρὸς ἄλληλα τῶν μερῶν διαφοράν, ἀλλὰ καὶ αὐτὰ τῇ πρὸς τὸ ἓν ἑαυτῆς ἀναφορᾷ τὰ μέρη, τῆς ἐν τῇ κλήσει διαφορᾶς ἀπολύουσα καὶ <669a> ταὐτὸν ἀλλήλοις ἄμφω δεικνύουσα καὶ θάτερον θατέρῳ κατ᾽ ἐπαλλαγὴν ὑπάρχον

---

[18] ὑφεστικότος CCSG
[19] δέχεται CCSG

are made one according to the same oneness[39] through faith. God
himself works this oneness by nature without confusion around the
substances of the things that are, alleviating and making identical
that which is different around them by the reference to and oneness
with himself as their cause and beginning and end,[40] as it has been   [205]
demonstrated.

(2) How and in What Mode the Holy Church is the Image of the Universe, which Subsists in Visible and Invisible[41] Realities

As the second point of his contemplation, the blessed elder said that
the holy Church of God is a representation and image of the entire
universe, which subsists in visible and invisible realities, because the   [CCSG 15]
Church contains the same oneness and diversity as God.

For, although the Church is one building according to its construction, she contains differences in the particularity of the physical   [210]
layout. She is divided into the place designated for priests and ministers alone (which we call the sanctuary), and the place accessible for
all the faithful people to enter (which we call the nave). But, again,
the Church is one in substance. The Church is not divided by her   [215]
parts on account of the difference of the parts themselves to one
another, but rather she dissolves the differences in name of the parts
themselves by her reference to the unity. She displays that both the
sanctuary and the nave are identical to one another and illustrates
that each one exists in the other according to exchange, although   [220]
each one is established by itself. The nave is identical to the sanctuary

[39]κατ᾽ αὐτήν; the presumed antecedent is "oneness" [ἔνωσιν]. Maximus is
therefore saying that God, who makes all things one, thereby rendering intellection
possible, works this same oneness in the Church though bringing people into community with one another.

[40]τέλος; the word has a rich array of meanings, including not only "end" as in
"termination" or "cessation" but also "end" as in "goal" or "final destiny."

[41]The distinction between "visible" [ὁρατός] and "invisible" [ἀόρατος] realities
is a clear echo of the Nicene Creed, which affirms in the first article that God is the
maker of all things, both visible and invisible. Although not precisely parallel, Maximus may also have Rom 1.20 in mind when he draws this distinction.

ὅπερ ἑκάτερον ἑαυτῷ καθέστηκεν ὂν ἀποφαίνουσα, ἱερατεῖον
μὲν τὸν ναὸν κατὰ τὴν δύναμιν, τῇ πρὸς τὸ πέρας ἀναφορᾷ τῆς
μυσταγωγίας ἱερουργούμενον, καὶ ἔμπαλιν ναὸν τὸ ἱερατεῖον
κατὰ τὴν ἐνέργειαν τῆς ἰδίας αὐτὸν²⁰ ἔχον μυσταγωγίας ἀρχήν,
μία δι' ἀμφοῖν καὶ ἡ αὐτὴ διαμένει.

Οὕτω καὶ ὁ ἐκ Θεοῦ κατὰ γένεσιν παρηγμένος σύμπας τῶν
ὄντων κόσμος, διαιρούμενος εἴς τε τὸν νοητὸν κόσμον, τὸν ἐκ
νοερῶν καὶ ἀσωμάτων οὐσιῶν συμπληρούμενον, καὶ τὸν αἰσθητὸν
τοῦτον καὶ σωματικὸν καὶ ἐκ πολλῶν μεγαλοφυῶς συνυφασμένον
εἰδῶν τε καὶ φύσεων, ἄλλη πως ὑπάρχων ἀχειροποίητος
Ἐκκλησία διὰ ταύτης τῆς χειροποιήτου σοφῶς ὑποφαίνεται,
καὶ <669b> ἱερατεῖον μὲν ὥσπερ ἔχων τὸν ἄνω κόσμον καὶ ταῖς
ἄνω προσνενεμημένον δυνάμεσι, ναὸν δέ, τὸν κάτω καὶ τοῖς
δι' αἰσθήσεως ζῆν λαχοῦσι προσκεχωρημένον. πάλιν εἷς ἐστι
κόσμος τοῖς ἑαυτοῦ μὴ συνδιαιρούμενος μέρεσι· τοὐναντίον δὲ
καὶ αὐτῶν τῶν μερῶν τὴν ἐξ ἰδιότητος φυσικῆς διαφοράν, τῇ
πρὸς τὸ ἓν ἑαυτοῦ καὶ ἀδιαίρετον ἀναφορᾷ περιγράφων, καὶ
ταὐτὸν ἑαυτῷ τε καὶ ἀλλήλοις ἀσυγχύτως ἐναλλὰξ ὄντας, καὶ
θατέρῳ θάτερον ὅλον ὅλῳ δεικνὺς ἐμβεβηκότα, καὶ ἄμφω ὅλον
αὐτὸν ὡς μέρη ἕνα συμπληροῦντας, καὶ κατ' αὐτὸν ὡς ὅλον μέρη
ἑνοειδῶς τε καὶ ὁλικῶς συμπληρουμένους. ὅλος γὰρ ὁ νοητὸς
<669c> κόσμος ὅλῳ τῷ αἰσθητῷ μυστικῶς τοῖς συμβολικοῖς εἴδεσι
τυπούμενος φαίνεται τοῖς ὁρᾶν δυναμένοις· καὶ ὅλος ὅλῳ τῷ
νοητῷ ὁ αἰσθητὸς γνωστικῶς κατὰ νοῦν τοῖς λόγοις ἁπλούμενος

---

²⁰ἰδίας αὐτὸν : ἀδιαστάτου CCSG
²¹ἐνυπάρχων ἐστίν : ἔνεστιν CCSG

according to power because it is consecrated by the anaphora[42] at the consummation of the mystagogy and, conversely, the sanctuary is identical to the nave according to activity because it is the place where the never-ending mystagogy begins. The Church remains one and the same through both.

In the same way, the entire universe of everything that is—which was brought forth from God at the creation and is divided into the intelligible realm,[43] which is comprised of intellectual and bodiless substance, and the realm that is sensible and bodily and which has been ingeniously interwoven[44] from many forms and natures, and which exists somehow as another Church that is made without hands—is seen in wisdom through this Church that is made with hands.[45] The universe possesses a sanctuary, which is the realm above and is assigned to the powers above, and it also possesses a nave, which is the realm below and is traversed by those whose lot it is to live through sense perception. Again, the universe is one, and it is not divided by its parts; conversely, it limits the difference of these parts in their particular natures by the reference to its own undivided unity. And these realms are alternately identical with the universe and are without confusion with one another. The universe demonstrates that the whole of each enters into the whole of the other, and both are the same whole:[46] as parts, the realms comprise one whole, and by itself as a whole, the realms are comprised of parts singly and wholly. For the whole intelligible realm, which is impressed mystically in sym-

[CCSG 16; 225]

[230]

[235]

[240]

[42]ἀναφορά; although this word is translated "reference" in earlier passages, for many centuries (perhaps as early as the fourth-century *Apostolic Constitutions*) the word has been used to designate that part of the Liturgy in which the bread and wine are consecrated. It can also mean "an offering" and, in Christian texts, "the Eucharistic offering" specifically. "Eucharist" is a possible alternative in this passage.

[43]Both "universe" and "realm" are translations of κόσμος.

[44]συνυφαίνω; Lampe observes that this word is used to describe the union of the two natures of Christ in Origen, *Contra Celsum* 3.28, and Epiphanius, *Panarion* 76.46. Maximus uses several such compound verbs in the surrounding context, including ἀποφαίνω ("she displays") in the previous sentence and ὑποφαίνω ("is seen") later on in the present sentence.

[45]Cf. Mk 14.58; Heb 9.11, 24.

[46]Maximus is speaking of the reciprocity of the intelligible and sensible realms.

ἐνυπάρχων ἐστίν.[21] ἐν ἐκείνῳ γὰρ οὗτος τοῖς λόγοις ἐστί, κἀκεῖνος ἐν τούτῳ τοῖς τύποις· καὶ τὸ ἔργον αὐτῶν ἕν,[22] καθὼς ἂν εἴη τροχὸς ἐν τῷ τροχῷ, φησὶν ὁ θαυμαστὸς τῶν μεγάλων θεατὴς Ἰεζεκιήλ, περὶ τῶν δύο κόσμων, οἶμαι,[23] λέγων. καὶ πάλιν· τὰ γὰρ ἀόρατα αὐτοῦ ἀπὸ κτίσεως κόσμου τοῖς ποιήμασι νοούμενα καθορᾶται, φησὶν ὁ θεῖος Ἀπόστολος. καὶ εἰ καθορᾶται διὰ τῶν φαινομένων τὰ μὴ φαινόμενα, καθὼς γέγραπται, πολλῷ δὴ καὶ[24] διὰ τῶν μὴ φαινομένων τοῖς θεωρίᾳ πνευματικῇ προσανέχουσι τὰ φαινόμενα νοηθήσεται. τῶν γὰρ νοητῶν ἡ διὰ τῶν ὁρατῶν συμβολικὴ <669d> θεωρία, τῶν ὁρομένων[25] ἐστὶ διὰ τῶν ἀοράτων πνευματικὴ ἐπιστήμη καὶ νόησις. δεῖ γὰρ τὰ ἀλλήλων ὄντα δηλωτικὰ πάντως ἀληθεῖς καὶ ἀριδήλους τὰς ἀλλήλων ἔχειν ἐμφάσεις καὶ τὴν ἐπ᾽ αὐταῖς σχέσιν ἀλώβητον.

<672a> **Κεφαλ. Γ. Ὅτι καὶ μόνου τοῦ αἰσθητοῦ κόσμου ἐστὶν εἰκὼν ἡ ἁγία τοῦ Θεοῦ Ἐκκλησία**

Καὶ αὖθις μόνου τοῦ αἰσθητοῦ κόσμου καθ᾽ ἑαυτὸν τὴν ἁγίαν τοῦ Θεοῦ Ἐκκλησίαν εἶναι σύμβολον ἔφασκεν, ὡς οὐρανὸν μὲν τὸ θεῖον ἱερατεῖον ἔχουσαν, γῆν δὲ τὴν εὐπρέπειαν τοῦ ναοῦ κεκτημένην. ὡσαύτως δὲ καὶ τὸν κόσμον ὑπάρχειν Ἐκκλησίαν· ἱερατείῳ μὲν ἐοικότα τὸν οὐρανὸν ἔχοντα, ναῷ δὲ τὴν κατὰ γῆν διακόσμησιν.

---

[22]ἦν CCSG
[23]ὡς οἶμαι CCSG
[24]που CCSG
[25]ὁρωμένων CCSG

bolic forms in the whole sensible realm, appears for those who are able to see, and the whole sensible realm, which is intellectually simplified into its principles according to the mind, exists in the whole intelligible realm. For, the sensible realm is in the intelligible realm in the principles, and the intelligible realm is in the sensible realm in the representations. "And their construction was just as if a wheel was within a wheel,"[47] says Ezekiel, the marvelous seer of great visions, which I suppose he spoke concerning the two realms. And again, the divine apostle says: "Ever since the creation of the world his invisible attributes have been clearly seen and apprehended in the things that have been made."[48] And if the things that do not appear "are clearly seen" through the things that appear, as it is written, how much more will the things that appear be perceived through the things that do not appear by those who devote themselves to spiritual contemplation. For the contemplation of the symbols of the intelligible things through the things that are visible is spiritual knowledge and intelligence of the things that are seen through the things that are invisible. For it is necessary that things that signify one another possess entirely true and distinct reflections of one another and an unbroken relationship with these reflections. [CCSG 17; 245] [250] [255]

(3) That The Holy Church of God Is The Image of The Sensible Realm Alone[49]

And the blessed elder again said that the holy Church of God is a symbol of the sensible realm alone and by itself because she possesses the divine sanctuary as heaven and attains the beautiful order of the nave as the earth. In the same way, he said that the sensible realm is a Church and possesses heaven, which is analogous to the sanctuary, and the orderly arrangement of the earth, which is analogous to the nave. [CCSG 18; 260]

[47]Ezek 1.16.
[48]Rom 1.20.
[49]This title could also be translated: "That the holy Church of God is the image of the sensible realm even when it is considered alone."

Κεφαλ. Δ. Πῶς τε καὶ ποίῳ τρόπῳ συμβολικῶς εἰκονίζει τὸν
ἄνθρωπον ἡ ἁγία τοῦ Θεοῦ Ἐκκλησία, καὶ αὐτὴ ὡς ἄνθρωπος ὑπ᾽
αὐτοῦ εἰκονίζεται

Καὶ πάλιν κατ᾽ ἄλλον τρόπον θεωρίας, ἄνθρωπον <672b> εἶναι τὴν
ἁγίαν τοῦ Θεοῦ Ἐκκλησίαν ἔλεγε, ψυχὴν μὲν ἔχουσαν τὸ ἱερατεῖον·
καὶ νοῦν τὸ θεῖον θυσιαστήριον, καὶ σῶμα τὸν ναόν, ὡς εἰκόνα
καὶ ὁμοίωσιν ὑπάρχουσαν τοῦ κατ᾽ εἰκόνα Θεοῦ καὶ ὁμοίωσιν
γενομένου ἀνθρώπου, καὶ διὰ μὲν τοῦ ναοῦ, ὡς διὰ σώματος,
τὴν ἠθικὴν φιλοσοφίαν προβαλλομένην, διὰ δὲ τοῦ ἱερατείου,
ὡς διὰ ψυχῆς, τὴν φυσικὴν θεωρίαν πνευματικῶς ἐξηγουμένην
καὶ ὡς διὰ νοὸς τοῦ θείου θυσιαστηρίου τὴν μυστικὴν θεολογίαν
ἐμβαίνουσαν.²⁶

Καὶ ἔμπαλιν Ἐκκλησίαν μυστικὴν τὸν ἄνθρωπον, ὡς διὰ ναοῦ
μὲν τοῦ σώματος τὸ πρακτικὸν τῆς ψυχῆς ταῖς τῶν ἐντολῶν
ἐνεργείαις κατὰ τὴν ἠθικὴν φιλοσοφίαν ἐναρέτως φαιδρύνοντα·
ὡς δι᾽ ἱερατείου δὲ τῆς ψυχῆς τοὺς κατ᾽ αἴσθησιν λόγους
<672c> καθαρῶς ἐν Πνεύματι τῆς ὕλης περιτμηθέντας κατὰ τὴν
φυσικὴν θεωρίαν διὰ λόγου τῷ Θεῷ προσκομίζοντα, καὶ ὡς διὰ
θυσιαστηρίου τοῦ νοός, τὴν ἐν ἀδύτοις πολυύμνητον τῆς ἀφανοῦς
καὶ ἀγνώστου μεγαλοφωνίας σιγὴν τῆς θεότητος δι᾽ ἄλλης λάλου
τε καὶ πολυφθόγγου σιγῆς προσκαλούμενον, καὶ ὡς ἐφικτὸν
ἀνθρώπῳ κατὰ μυστικὴν θεολογίαν αὐτῇ συγγινόμενον, καὶ
τοιοῦτον γινόμενον οἷον εἰκὸς εἶναι δεῖ τὸν ἐπιδημίας ἀξιωθέντα
Θεοῦ, καὶ ταῖς αὐτοῦ παμφαέσιν αἴγλαις ἐνσημανθέντα.

---

²⁶ἐμφαίνουσαν CCSG

(4) How and in What Mode the Holy Church of God Symbolically Images a Human Being and, as a Human Being, is Imaged by a Human Being

And again, according to another mode of his contemplation, he said that the holy Church of God is a human being, which has the sanctuary as its soul, the divine altar as its mind, and the nave as its body. [265] And therefore the Church is as the image and likeness of a human being who was made "according to the image" and "likeness of God."[50] The Church sets forth moral discipline through the nave as through the body, and spiritually interprets natural contemplation[51] through the sanctuary as through the soul, and reveals mystical theology[52] through the divine altar as through the mind. [270]

And, conversely, he said that man is a mystical Church—through the body as through the nave, man virtuously cleanses the practical [CCSG 19] part of the soul by the outworking of the commandments according to moral discipline. Through the soul as through the sanctuary, [275] man brings to God through reason the principles according to sense perception that have been circumcised of matter purely and by the Spirit according to natural contemplation. And through the mind as through the altar, man summons by means of another kind silence—one that is composed of many syllables and notes—the often-sung "silence in the inner sanctuaries"[53] of the unseen and unknowable majestic voice of divinity.[54] And, in as far as it is pos- [280] sible for man, he becomes acquainted with the silence according to mystical theology and becomes such as one who has been made worthy of the visitation of God ought to be and is imprinted with his radiant splendor.

[50]Gen 1.27, 26.

[51]For Maximus, natural contemplation is beholding the physical world in order to enter into a deeper reflection of the spiritual principles thereby represented.

[52]Mystical theology is the intimate communion with God for which the ascetic Christian strives.

[53]Pseudo-Dionysius, *On the Divine Names* 4.22.

[54]This is a marvelous example of Maximus' appeal to paradox: the worshiper's song summons the silence that expresses the unknowable voice of God!

Κεφαλ. Ε. Πῶς καὶ ποίῳ τρόπῳ πάλιν τῆς ψυχῆς καθ᾽ ἑαυτὴν νοουμένης εἰκών τε καὶ τύπος[27] ἡ ἁγία τοῦ <672d> Θεοῦ Ἐκκλησία

Καὶ οὐχ ὅλου μὲν τοῦ ἀνθρώπου, τοῦ ἐκ ψυχῆς καὶ σώματος κατὰ σύνθεσίν φημι συνεστῶτος, εἰκόνα μόνον εἶναι δύνασθαι τὴν ἁγίαν Ἐκκλησίαν ἐδίδασκεν, ἀλλὰ καὶ αὐτῆς τῆς ψυχῆς καθ᾽ ἑαυτὴν τῷ λόγῳ θεωρουμένης. Ἐπειδὴ γὰρ ἐκ νοερᾶς καὶ ζωτικῆς δυνάμεως καθολικῶς συνίστασθαι τὴν ψυχὴν ἔφασκε· καὶ τῆς μὲν νοερᾶς ἐξουσιαστικῶς κατὰ βούλησιν κινουμένης, τῆς δὲ ζωτικῆς κατὰ φύσιν ἀπροαιρέτως, ὡς ἔχει, μενούσης.

Καὶ πάλιν, τῆς μὲν νοερᾶς εἶναι τό τε θεωρητικόν, καὶ τὸ πρακτικόν· καὶ τὸ μὲν θεωρητικὸν καλεῖσθαι νοῦν ἔλεγε· τὸ δὲ πρακτικόν, λόγον· καὶ τῆς μὲν νοερᾶς δυνάμεως <673a> κινητικὸν εἶναι τὸν νοῦν, τῆς δὲ ζωτικῆς προνοητικὸν ὑπάρχειν τὸν λόγον· καὶ τὸν μὲν εἶναί τε καὶ καλεῖσθαι σοφίαν, φημὶ δὲ τὸν νοῦν, ὅταν παντάπασιν ἀτρέπτους ἑαυτοῦ διαφυλάττῃ τὰς πρὸς τὸν Θεὸν κινήσεις· τὸν δὲ λόγον ὡσαύτως φρόνησιν καὶ εἶναι καὶ καλεῖσθαι, ὅταν σωφρόνως τὴν ὑπ᾽ αὐτοῦ κατὰ πρόνοιαν διοικουμένην ζωτικὴν δύναμιν ταῖς ἐνεργείαις συνάψας τῷ νῷ δείξειεν ἀδιάφορον· τὴν αὐτὴν αὐτῷ καὶ ὁμοίαν δι᾽ ἀρετῆς ἔμφασιν τοῦ θείου φέρουσαν, ἣν καὶ ἐπιμερίζεσθαι τῷ τε νῷ καὶ τῷ λόγῳ φυσικῶς ἔλεγεν· ὡς εἶναι μᾶλλον καὶ συνισταμένη δείκνυσθαι προηγουμένως τὴν ψυχὴν ἐκ τοῦ νοῦ καὶ τοῦ λόγου, ὡς νοεράν τε καὶ λογικήν· τῆς ζωτικῆς ἐπ᾽ ἀμφοῖν κατὰ τὸ ἴσον δηλονότι, νοῦ τε καὶ λόγου φημί, θεωρουμένης δυνάμεως· οὐδ᾽ ὁπότερον <673b> γὰρ τούτων ζωῆς ἄμοιρον εἶναι θέμις ἐννοεῖν

---

[27]τύπος : τύπος ἐστίν CCSG

(5) How and in What Mode, again, the Holy Church of God is the Image and Representation also of the Soul When Considered on Its Own

Furthermore, the blessed elder taught that the holy Church is not only able to be the image of the whole human being (I am speaking [285] about man who is comprised of soul and body in union) but also of the soul itself, when contemplated on its own by reason. He said then [CCSG 20] that the soul is comprised in total of an intellectual and an animate power: the intellectual power, which moves by self-determination according to its own will, and the animate power, which remains as [290] it is according to nature by lack of choice.

And, again, he said that both the contemplative and the practical parts belong to the intellectual power, and that the contemplative part is called the mind, whereas the practical part is called reason. The mind is the part that causes motion in the intellectual power, [295] while reason is the part that is provident[55] in the animate power. It is and is called wisdom (I am speaking now about the mind) whenever it completely keeps its own motions unchangeably towards God.[56] In the same way, reason is and is called prudence whenever by discretion it demonstrates itself to be no different from the mind [300] because it joins the animate power (which reason controls according to providence) to the activities, and the animate power bears an identical and equal reflection of the divine as the mind through virtue. And he said that the animate power is assigned to the mind and reason by nature, since the soul has been demonstrated in its essence to consist of or rather to be mind and reason (because it is intellectual and rational) and the animate power (because it is contemplated by both equally—I am speaking of the mind and reason,

[55]προνοητικός; this word means "taking care for" or "showing forethought for." However, the term also carries clear etymological links to νοῦς ("mind") and νοερός ("intellectual").

[56]Maximus seems to be saying that whenever the motions of our mind remain unchangeably directed towards God, then the mind can be called wisdom because it finds fulfillment in arriving upon the being whom it was created to contemplate.

καὶ ὑπ᾽ ἀμφοῖν διειλημμένης, δι᾽ ἧς ὁ μὲν νοῦς, ὃν καὶ σοφίαν ἔφαμεν καλεῖσθαι, τῇ θεωρητικῇ ἕξει κατ᾽ ἀπόρρητον σιγήν τε καὶ γνῶσιν ἐξαπλούμενος πρὸς τὴν ἀλήθειαν δι᾽ ἀλήστου τε καὶ ἀκαταλήκτου γνώσεως ἄγεται, ὁ δὲ λόγος, ὃν ἐκαλέσαμεν φρόνησιν, τῇ πρακτικῇ ἕξει σωματικῶς²⁸ κατ᾽ ἀρετὴν εἰς τὸ ἀγαθὸν διὰ πίστεως καταλήγει· ἐξ ὧν ἀμφοτέρων ἡ ἀληθὴς τῶν τε²⁹ θείων καὶ τῶν ἀνθρωπίνων ἐπιστήμη συνέστηκε πραγμάτων, ἡ ὄντως ἄπταιστος γνῶσις καὶ πάσης τῆς κατὰ Χριστιανοὺς θειοτάτης φιλοσοφίας πέρας.

<673c> Καὶ σαφέστερον περὶ τούτων εἰπεῖν, τῆς ψυχῆς τὸ μὲν ἔλεγε εἶναι θεωρητικόν, καθὼς εἴρηται, τὸ δὲ πρακτικόν· καὶ τὸ μὲν θεωρητικὸν ἐκάλει νοῦν, τὸ δὲ πρακτικόν, λόγον, ὡς πρώτας δηλαδὴ³⁰ δυνάμεις τῆς ψυχῆς· καὶ πάλιν τὸν νοῦν, σοφίαν, τὸν δὲ λόγον, φρόνησιν, ὡς πρώτας ἐνεργείας.

Διεξοδικῶς δὲ πάλιν τῆς ψυχῆς ἔφασκεν εἶναι, κατὰ μὲν τὸ νοερόν, τὸν νοῦν, τὴν σοφίαν, τὴν θεωρίαν, τὴν γνῶσιν, τὴν ἄληστον γνῶσιν, τούτων δὲ τέλος εἶναι τὴν ἀλήθειαν· κατὰ δὲ τὸ λογικόν, τὸν λόγον, τὴν φρόνησιν, τὴν πρᾶξιν, τὴν ἀρετήν, τὴν πίστιν, τούτων δὲ τέλος εἶναι τὸ ἀγαθόν. τὴν ἀλήθειαν δὲ καὶ τὸ

---

²⁸σωματικῶς : σωστικῶς CCSG
²⁹om. CCSG
³⁰δηλονότι CCSG

for it is not proper to consider that either of these are without a share [CCSG 21] of life[57]—and comprehended by both). Through the animate power, the mind, which we said is also called wisdom, when it is explained[58] [310] in the contemplative habit according to the ineffable silence and knowledge, is led to the truth through "unforgettable" and incessant "knowledge." And through the animate power, reason, which we called prudence, comes to an end salvifically in the good through faith by the practical habit according to virtue.[59] From both the mind and reason, true expertise of divine and human realities unite, [315] a knowledge which is actually infallible knowledge and the end of every divine philosophy according to Christians.

To speak more clearly about these things, the blessed elder said that the soul possesses a contemplative part and a practical part, even as I said above. The contemplative part he called the mind, and [320] the practical part he called reason, since they are clearly the primary [CCSG 22] powers of the soul. And, again, the mind he called wisdom, and reason he called understanding, since they are the primary activities of the soul.

And, again, in more detail, he said that, according to the intellectual part, the soul possesses the mind, wisdom, contemplation, knowledge, and "ceaseless knowledge;"[60] truth is the end of these [325] things. And, according to the rational part, the soul possesses reason, prudence, practice, virtue, and faith; the good is the end of these things. Truth and the good, he said, reveal God: truth reveals

---

[57]The logic of Maximus' deduction turns on the etymological relationship of the Greek terms ζωή ("life") and ζωός ("animate"). The animate power is assigned to both the mind and reason, and so is not reasonable that either the mind or reason should be without life.

[58]ἐξαπλόω; the word means "to explain" or "unfold" and is a compound form of ἁπλόω, which means "to be simple" or "to make one." In Maximus' mind, intellection is the process by which the many are made one; we therefore correctly understand something when we perceive the unity in any particular complex reality. Because it is God who unifies everything, every act of intellection is an encounter with God.

[59]Maximus is saying that our reason is sanctified through the practice of virtues.

[60]Pseudo-Dionysius, *On the Divine Names* 4.35.

ἀγαθόν, τὸν Θεὸν ἔλεγε δηλοῦν, ἀλλὰ τὴν μὲν ἀλήθειαν, ὅταν ἐκ τῆς οὐσίας τὸ θεῖον σημαίνεσθαι δοκῇ· ἁπλοῦν γάρ, καὶ μόνον, καὶ ἕν, καὶ ταυτόν, καὶ <673d> ἀμερές, καὶ ἄτρεπτον, καὶ ἀπαθὲς πρᾶγμα ἡ ἀλήθεια καὶ ἀλάθητον, καὶ παντελῶς ἀδιάστατον· τὸ δὲ ἀγαθόν, ὅταν ἐκ τῆς ἐνεργείας. Εὐεργετικὸν γὰρ τὸ ἀγαθόν, καὶ προνοητικὸν τῶν ἐξ αὐτοῦ πάντων, καὶ φρουρητικόν, ἀπὸ τοῦ³¹ ἄγαν εἶναι, ἢ τεθεῖσθαι ἢ θέειν, κατὰ τὴν τῶν ἐτυμολογούντων δόξαν, πᾶσι τοῖς οὖσι τοῦ εἶναι³² καὶ διαμένειν καὶ κινεῖσθαι χαριστικόν.

<676a> Τὰς οὖν περὶ τὴν ψυχὴν νοουμένας πέντε συζυγίας περὶ τὴν μίαν τὴν τοῦ Θεοῦ σημαντικὴν συζυγίαν ἔλεγε καταγίνεσθαι. συζυγίαν³³ δέ φημι νῦν τὸν νοῦν καὶ τὸν λόγον, τὴν σοφίαν καὶ τὴν φρόνησιν, τὴν θεωρίαν καὶ τὴν πρᾶξιν, τὴν γνῶσιν καὶ τὴν ἀρετήν, τὴν ἄληστον γνῶσιν καὶ τὴν πίστιν. τὴν δὲ τοῦ θείου σημαντικήν, τὴν ἀλήθειαν καὶ τὸ ἀγαθόν· αἷς κατὰ πρόοδον ἡ ψυχὴ κινουμένη, τῷ Θεῷ τῶν ὅλων ἑνοῦται, μιμουμένη αὐτοῦ τῆς οὐσίας καὶ τῆς ἐνεργείας τὸ ἄτρεπτον καὶ εὐεργετικόν, διὰ τῆς ἐν τῷ καλῷ παγίας καὶ ἀμεταθέτου κατὰ τὴν προαίρεσιν ἕξεως.

Καί, ἵνα τούτων μικρόν τι μίξω θεώρημα πρόσφορον, τάχα αὕτη ἐστὶν ἡ θεία δεκὰς τῶν χορδῶν τοῦ κατὰ ψυχὴν νοητοῦ ψαλτηρίου, ἡ τὸν λόγον ὑπηχοῦντα τῷ Πνεύματι διὰ τῆς ἄλλης τῶν ἐντολῶν μακαρίας <676b> δεκάδος ἔχουσα, καὶ τοὺς ἐντελεῖς τε καὶ ἁρμονίους καὶ ἐμμελεῖς³⁴ νοητῶς ἀποτελοῦσα φθόγγους,

---

³¹ἀπὸ τοῦ : καὶ τῷ CCSG
³²εἶναί τε CCSG
³³συζυγίαν : συζυγίας CCSG
³⁴εὐμελεῖς CCSG

God whenever the divine seems to be signified from existence, for truth is a simple, solitary, unified, identical, indivisible, unchangeable, passionless, inescapable, and absolutely eternal reality; and the good reveals God whenever the divine seems to be signified from activity, for the good is beneficent, provident, and watchful over everything that comes from it.[61] And, according to the opinion of the etymologists, the good is that which abundantly exists or is situated or runs, for it bestows existence and permanence and movement to everything that is.[62]

[330]

[335]

Then he said that the five pairs[63] of the soul that we discussed above are parallel to the pair that signifies the divine. The pairs of which I am now speaking are the mind and reason, wisdom and prudence, contemplation and practice, knowledge and virtue, "ceaseless knowledge"[64] and faith. Truth and the good are the pair that signifies the divine. And when the soul is moved by progression in the above-mentioned pairs, and when the soul imitates the unchangeability and beneficence of God's being and activity through steadfastness to the good and the immutability of its habit according to choice,[65] it is united to the God of all things.

[CCSG 23]

[340]

[345]

And, if I might add to these things one small, useful contemplation: perhaps these five pairs are the divine decad—the ten strings of the intelligible harp[66] of the soul. The five pairs contain the word that resounds in the Spirit through the other blessed decad of the ten commandments, and they perform in an intelligible manner[67] the

[350]

[61]The personal pronoun we have here translated "it" could also be translated "him," in which case God would be the antecedent.

[62]Maximus' observation is that the etymologists claim that the adjective "good" [ἀγαθόν] derives from the adverb "in abundance" [ἄγαν].

[63]συζυγία is yet another word in Maximus' vocabulary that can mean "union."

[64]Pseudo-Dionysius, *On the Divine Names* 4.35.

[65]That is, when the soul makes progress in its motion toward the above-mentioned virtues, and when the soul imitates the immutability of God in the habits it has developed through choosing virtue consistently.

[66]Cf. Ps 32.2; 143.9.

[67]νοητῶς; the ten virtues discussed above pertain to the intelligible realm as the ten commandments pertain to the sensible realm.

δι᾽ ὧν ὑμνεῖται ὁ Θεός. ἵν᾽ ἐγὼ μάθω, τίς ὁ τῆς ᾀδούσης καὶ[35] τῆς ᾀδομένης δεκάδος ὁ[36] λόγος, καὶ πῶς δεκάδι δεκὰς μυστικῶς ἑνουμένη τε καὶ συναπτομένη, Ἰησοῦν μὲν τὸν ἐμὸν Θεὸν καὶ Σωτῆρα συμπληρωθέντα δι᾽ ἐμοῦ σωζομένου, πρὸς ἑαυτὸν ἐπανάγει τὸν ἀεὶ πληρέστατον[37] καὶ μηδέποτε ἑαυτοῦ ἐκστῆναι δυνάμενον, ἐμὲ δὲ τὸν ἄνθρωπον[38] θαυμαστῶς ἑαυτῷ[39] ἀποκαθίστησι, μᾶλλον δὲ Θεῷ, παρ᾽ οὗ τὸ εἶναι λαβὼν ἔχω, καὶ πρὸς ὃν ἐπείγομαι, πόρρωθεν τὸ εὖ εἶναι προσλαβεῖν ἐφιέμενος. ὅπερ ὁ γνῶναι δυνηθείς, ἐκ τοῦ παθεῖν τὰ λεγόμενα εἴσεται πάντως γνωρίσας ἤδη κατὰ τὴν πεῖραν ἐναργῶς τὸ οἰκεῖον ἀξίωμα, πῶς ἀποδίδοται τῇ εἰκόνι τὸ κατ᾽ εἰκόνα, πῶς[40] <676c> τιμᾶται τὸ ἀρχέτυπον, τίς[41] τοῦ μυστηρίου τῆς ἡμῶν σωτηρίας ἡ δύναμις, καὶ ὑπὲρ τίνος Χριστὸς ἀπέθανε· πῶς τε πάλιν ἐν αὐτῷ μεῖναι

---

[35]καὶ : καὶ τίς ὁ CCSG
[36]om. CCSG
[37]πληρέστατόν τε καὶ ὑπερπληρέστατον CCSG
[38]ἄνθρωπον ἐμαυτῷ CCSG
[39]om. CCSG
[40]πῶς : καὶ πῶς CCSG
[41]καὶ τίς CCSG

majestic[68], harmonious, and melodious notes, through which God is praised in song. And this is so in order that I might learn what[69] is the word of the singing decad[70] and what is the word of the sung decad,[71] and how a decad is mystically made one with and joined to another decad.[72] On the one hand, the decad draws me back to him[73]—Jesus, my God and Savior, the one who is fulfilled[74] through me (the one [355] who is being saved) and yet one who is always full and always over-flowing[75] and never able to deplete himself. But on the other hand, [CCSG 24] the decad marvelously restores me—the man[76]—to myself, or rather to God, from whom I received and now possess being and to whom I am driven from afar, longing also to receive well-being.[77] The one [360] who is able to learn from experience will certainly know what we are speaking about, because he will have already clearly "recognized" from experience the "dignity" that is proper to him, how "it

[68]ἐντελής; the word literally means "complete, full." The word bears an affinity to the word ἐντέλλω ("to command") and therefore appears to be a natural word choice to describe a command (ἐντολή).

[69]In Greek, this pronoun could also be translated "who," and so this could be a Christological reference.

[70]I.e., the decad of the five pairs of virtues in the soul.

[71]I.e., the decad of the ten commandments.

[72]Maximus teaches that God delivers the same message in the ten virtues and in the ten commandments. The ten virtues are, presumably, the "singing decad," given the active role in the metaphor assumed by the ten strings of the harp as the source of sound. The "sung decad" is then the ten commandments.

[73]ἑαυτόν; this term could also be translated "himself," and therefore Maximus may intend a Christological reference in this context as well. The decad is this summary of God's revelatory message (the λόγος) expressed in both the sensible realm by the ten commandments and the intelligible realm by the ten virtues.

[74]συμπληρόω; this word could also be translated "fulfilled together." Maximus is saying that Jesus is fulfilled together with us, and so we partake in God's nature in our salvation.

[75]"Full" and "overflowing" are superlative adjectives in the Greek text, as if to say "full and overflowing to the uttermost!" We should note that Maximus is constructing a wordplay with the verb συμπληρόω and the adjectives πλήρης and ὑπερπλήρης: although Jesus is fulfilled through us, he is the one who is always full and never in need of filling.

[76]"Man" is clearly parallel to "Savior" from the line above. In fact, these several lines could be readily placed into a chiasm.

[77]Cf. Pseudo-Dionysius, *Ecclesiastical Hierarchy* 1.3.

δυνάμεθα, καὶ αὐτὸς ἐν ἡμῖν, καθὼς εἶπε, καὶ πῶς ἐστιν εὐθὺς ὁ λόγος τοῦ Κυρίου, καὶ πάντα τὰ ἔργα αὐτοῦ ἐν πίστει.

Ἀλλ᾽ ἐπανάγωμεν πρὸς τὸν εἱρμὸν τοῦ λόγου τὸν λόγον, τούτοις περὶ τούτων ἀρκεσθέντες.

Τὸν γὰρ νοῦν διὰ τῆς σοφίας ἔφασκε κινούμενον, εἰς θεωρίαν ἱέναι· διὰ δὲ τῆς θεωρίας, εἰς γνῶσιν· διὰ δὲ τῆς γνώσεως, εἰς τὴν ἄληστον γνῶσιν· διὰ δὲ τῆς ἀλήστου γνώσεως, εἰς τὴν ἀλήθειαν· περὶ ἣν ὁ νοῦς ὅρον τῆς κινήσεως δέχεται, περιγραφομένης <676d> αὐτῷ[42] τῆς τε οὐσίας καὶ τῆς δυνάμεως καὶ τῆς ἕξεως καὶ τῆς ἐνεργείας. νοῦ γὰρ ἔλεγε δύναμιν εἶναι τὴν σοφίαν, καὶ αὐτὸν εἶναι τὸν νοῦν δυνάμει σοφίαν· τὴν δὲ θεωρίαν, ἕξιν· τὴν δὲ γνῶσιν, ἐνέργειαν· τὴν δὲ ἄληστον γνῶσιν, σοφίας τε καὶ θεωρίας καὶ γνώσεως, ἤγουν δυνάμεως καὶ ἕξεως καὶ ἐνεργείας, τὴν περὶ <677a> τὸ γνωστὸν τὸ ὑπὲρ πᾶσαν τὴν[43] γνῶσιν ἀκατάληκτον καὶ ἑκτικὴν ἀεικινησίαν, ἧς πέρας ἐστίν, ὡς ἀλάθητον γνωστόν, ἡ ἀλήθεια· ὃ καὶ θαυμάζειν ἄξιον, πῶς τὸ ἄληστον λήγει περιγραφόμενον, ἢ δηλονότι[44] ὡς Θεῷ τῇ ἀληθείᾳ περατούμενον· Θεὸς γὰρ ἡ ἀλήθεια περὶ ὃν ἀκαταλήκτως τε καὶ ἀλήστως κινούμενος ὁ νοῦς, λήγειν οὐκ ἔχει ποτὲ τῆς κινήσεως, μὴ εὑρίσκων πέρας ἔνθα μὴ ἔστι διάστημα. τὸ γὰρ θαυμαστὸν μέγεθος τῆς θείας ἀπειρίας ἄποσόν

[42]αὐτοῦ CCSG
[43]om. CCSG
[44]δῆλον CCSG

is given back to the image what is made after the image," and how "the archetype is honored," and what is "the power of the mystery" of our salvation, "and for whom Christ died,"[78] and how, again, we [365] are able "to abide in him" and "he in us,"[79] even as the Scripture says, and how "the word of the Lord is upright and all of his works are in faithfulness."[80]

But let us return the discourse to its outline, for these things suffice for the moment.

For, the blessed elder said that the mind, when moved through [370] wisdom, enters into contemplation, and through contemplation into knowledge, and through knowledge into "ceaseless knowledge,"[81] and through "ceaseless knowledge"[82] into truth. The mind receives the end of its motion in truth, because truth defines the limits of the mind's essence and power and habit and activity. For he said that [375] wisdom is a power of the mind, and that the mind itself is wisdom in power, and that contemplation is habit in power, and that knowledge [CCSG 25] is activity in power. And "ceaseless knowledge" is ceaseless motion, the incessant and habitual motion of wisdom and contemplation [380] and knowledge (that is to say, of power and habit and activity) that is beyond the known and above all knowledge, and its limit is the truth as that which is inescapably known. And, this merits our wonder, how that which is unforgettable[83] comes to an end when it is limited or concluded in truth, that is, in God. For God is truth,[84] and because the mind is incessantly and unforgettably[85] moved around him, its motion does not come to an end, because it does not find a

---

[78]Gregory of Nazianzus, *Oration* 1.4 (trans. Harrison, p. 58).

[79]Jn 15.4.

[80]Ps 32.4.

[81]Pseudo-Dionysius, *On the Divine Names* 4.35.

[82]Ibid.

[83]In saying "that which is unforgettable," Maximus is referring to "that which is inescapably known" from the prior sentence.

[84]θεὸς γάρ ἡ ἀλήθεια; because "truth" is the articular noun, it seems that the Greek text should be translated: "the truth is God."

[85]Our minds are incessantly moved around God, and so it is impossible for our minds to forget God.

τί[45] ἐστι καὶ ἀμερὲς καὶ παντελῶς ἀδιάστατον, καὶ τὴν οἱανοῦν πρὸς τὸ γνωσθῆναι, ὅ τί ποτέ ἐστι κατ᾽ οὐσίαν, φθάνουσαν αὐτὸν οὐκ ἔχον κατάληψιν. τὸ δὲ μὴ ἔχον διάστημα ἢ κατάληψιν καθ᾽ ὁτιοῦν οὐκ ἔστι τινὶ περατόν.

<677b> Τὸν δὲ λόγον ὡσαύτως διὰ τῆς φρονήσεως κινούμενον εἰς τὴν πρᾶξιν ἰέναι, διὰ δὲ τῆς πράξεως εἰς ἀρετήν, διὰ δὲ τῆς ἀρετῆς, εἰς τὴν πίστιν, τὴν ὄντως βεβαίαν καὶ ἄπτωτον τῶν θείων πληροφορίαν· ἣν πρώτην ἔχων δυνάμει κατὰ τὴν φρόνησιν ὁ λόγος, ὕστερον ἐνεργείᾳ κατὰ τὴν ἀρετὴν ἐπιδείκνυται, διὰ τὴν ἐπ᾽ ἔργων[46] φανέρωσιν. ἡ γὰρ χωρὶς ἔργων πίστις νεκρόν τι,[47] καθὼς γέγραπται· πᾶν δὲ νεκρὸν καὶ ἀνενέργητον, οὐκ ἄν ποτέ τις εὖ φρονῶν τοῖς καλοῖς εἶναι θαρσήσειεν εἰπεῖν ἐνάριθμον. διὰ δὲ τῆς πίστεως εἰς τὸ ἀγαθόν, περὶ ὃ δέχεται τέλος, παυόμενος τῶν οἰκείων ἐνεργειῶν ὁ λόγος, περιγραφομένης αὐτοῦ τῆς τε δυνάμεως καὶ τῆς ἕξεως καὶ τῆς ἐνεργείας.

Λόγου γὰρ ἔφασκεν εἶναι δύναμιν τὴν φρόνησιν· <677c> καὶ αὐτὸν εἶναι δυνάμει τὸν λόγον, φρόνησιν· ἕξιν δέ, τὴν πρᾶξιν· ἐνέργειαν δέ, τὴν ἀρετήν· τὴν δὲ πίστιν φρονήσεώς τε καὶ πράξεως καὶ ἀρετῆς, ἤγουν δυνάμεως ἕξεώς τε καὶ ἐνεργείας, ἐνδιάθετον πῆξιν καὶ ἀναλλοίωτον· ἧς πέρας ἔσχατόν ἐστι τὸ ἀγαθόν, περὶ ὃ καταλήγων τῆς κινήσεως ὁ λόγος παύεται. Θεὸς γάρ ἐστι τὸ ἀγαθόν, ᾧ πέφυκε πᾶσα καὶ παντὸς λόγου περατοῦσθαι δύναμις.

---

[45]τέ CCSG
[46]ἔργοις CCSG
[47]νεκρόν τι : νεκρά CCSG

limit where there is no dimension. For the wonderful greatness of [385] the divine limitlessness is without quantity, without parts, and completely dimensionless, and in order that we should know whatever this limitlessness is in its essence, this limitlessness arrives at the greatness that cannot be comprehended.[86] And because the greatness has no dimension and cannot be comprehended, it is therefore not navigable[87] by anyone.

And, again, the blessed elder said that reason, when moved through [390] understanding, enters into practice, through practice into virtue, and through virtue into faith, which is truly the firm and infallible certainty about divine things.[88] Reason has this certainty first in power according to prudence, and it is demonstrated lastly in activity according to virtue in the manifestation of works—for "faith apart from works [395] is dead,"[89] as it has been written, and no one who thinks correctly [CCSG 26] would ever venture to say that anything dead and ineffective should be counted among the beautiful. And reason enters through faith into the good, where it receives its end and ceases from its own activities, because the limits of its power, habit, and activity are defined. For he [400] said that prudence is a power of reason and reason itself is prudence in power, practice is habit in power, and virtue is activity in power. And the faith that comes from prudence, conduct, and virtue—that is to say, from power, habit, and activity—is the inner and unchangeable stabil- [405] ity, whose farthest limit is the good, and reason comes to an end and ceases from motion around the good. For God is the good,[90] in whom every power of every reason is limited by nature.

[86]Maximus here summarizes his theological quest in a single paradox: we seek to know God, but God is infinite and we are finite, and so any true knowledge of God should be impossible.

[87]περατός; this word is clearly related to πέρας ("boundary"). It seems that when the boundaries of something are known, it becomes navigable.

[88]The terms βέβαιος ("firm") and πληροφορία ("certainty") are certainly favorite terms of the author of the Epistle to the Hebrews (see 2.2, 3.14, 6.19, 9.17 and 6.11, 10.22, respectively), and yet the above line from Maximus does not echo any one specific passage from Hebrews.

[89]Jas 2.26.

[90]θεὸς γάρ ἐστι τὸ ἀγαθόν; because "good" is the articular noun, it seems that the sentence should be translated: "the good is God."

Πῶς δὲ καὶ τίνα τρόπον τούτων ἕκαστον κατορθοῦται καὶ εἰς ἐνέργειαν ἄγεται, καὶ τίνα τούτων ἑκάστῳ ἠναντίωται ἢ προσῳκείωται καὶ ἐπὶ πόσον, διαιρεῖν τε καὶ λέγειν, οὐ τῆς παρούσης ἐστὶν ὑποθέσεως, πλὴν τοῦ ὅσον γιγνώσκειν, ὅτι πᾶσα ψυχὴ ἡνίκα διὰ τῆς χάριτος τοῦ ἁγίου Πνεύματος καὶ τῆς οἰκείας φιλοπονίας καὶ σπουδῆς ἀλλήλοις ταῦτα συνάψαι τε καὶ <677d> ἱστουργῆσαι δυνηθῇ—τὸν λόγον φημὶ τῷ νῷ, καὶ τῇ σοφίᾳ τὴν φρόνησιν, καὶ τῇ θεωρίᾳ τὴν πρᾶξιν, καὶ τῇ γνώσει τὴν ἀρετήν, καὶ τῇ ἀλήστῳ γνώσει τὴν πίστιν, οὐδενὸς ἐλαττουμένου πρὸς τὸ ἕτερον ἢ πλεονάζοντος, πάσης αὐτοῖς περικοπείσης ὑπερβολῆς καὶ ἐλλείψεως, καί, ἵνα συνελὼν εἴπω, μονάδα τὴν ἑαυτῆς δεκάδα ποιῆσαι—τηνικαῦτα καὶ αὐτὴ τῷ Θεῷ <680a> ἀληθινῷ τε καὶ ἀγαθῷ καὶ ἑνὶ καὶ μόνῳ ἑνωθήσεται, καλή τε καὶ μεγαλοπρεπής, καὶ αὐτῷ [κατὰ τὸ ἐφικτὸν][48] ἐμφερὴς γενομένη τῇ συμπληρώσει τῶν τεσσάρων γενικῶν ἀρετῶν τῶν δηλωτικῶν μὲν τῆς κατὰ ψυχὴν θείας δεκάδος, περιεκτικῶν δὲ τῆς ἄλλης τῶν ἐντολῶν μακαρίας δεκάδος. δεκὰς γὰρ δυνάμει ἐστὶν ἡ τετράς, ἀπὸ τῆς μονάδος εἱρμῷ κατὰ πρόοδον συντιθεμένη. καὶ πάλιν μονὰς ἡ αὐτή, κατὰ σύνοδον τὸ ἀγαθὸν μοναδικῶς περιέχουσα, καὶ τὸ ἁπλοῦν καὶ ἀμερὲς τῆς θείας ἐνεργείας ἐφ᾽ ἑαυτῆς ἀτμήτως μεμερισμένον δεικνύουσα· αἷς τὸ μὲν οἰκεῖον εὐτόνως ἀπαρεγχείρητον ἡ ψυχὴ διετήρησεν,[49] τὸ δὲ ἀλλότριον ἀνδρικῶς ὡς πονηρὸν ἀπερράπισεν, ὡς νοῦν εὔλογον ἔχουσα καὶ σοφίαν ἔμφρονα καὶ θεωρίαν ἔμπρακτον, καὶ γνῶσιν <680b> ἐνάρετον, καὶ τὴν ἐπ᾽ αὐταῖς[50] ἄληστον γνῶσιν πιστοτάτην ὁμοῦ καὶ ἀμετάπτωτον, καὶ ὡς τοῖς αἰτίοις τὰ αἰτιατά, καὶ ταῖς δυνάμεσι τὰς ἐνεργείας σωφρόνως συνημμένας Θεῷ προσκομίσασα, καὶ ἀντιλαβοῦσα τούτων τὴν ποιητικὴν τῆς ἁπλότητος θέωσιν.

---

[48]Without brackets CCSG
[49]διετήρησεν : διετήρησεν ἀγαθόν CCSG
[50]ἐπ᾽ αὐταῖς : ἐπὶ ταύταις CCSG

But it does not pertain to the present subject to define and to say how and in what mode each of these things is accomplished and led into activity and what is opposed to or associated with each [410] of these things and to what extent, except to the extent of knowing that when[91] every soul is able, through the grace of the Holy Spirit and its own hard work and diligence, to join and weave these things to one another—that is, reason to the mind, prudence to wisdom, [415] practice to contemplation, virtue to knowledge, and faith to "ceaseless knowledge"; and when none of these is inferior or superior to the other, and every superiority and inferiority among them is [CCSG 27] eliminated, and, if I may speak concisely, the soul's decad becomes a monad—then the soul is also made one with the true and good and [420] one and only God. And the soul becomes beautiful and magnificent and, as far as it is possible, like him by fulfilling the four cardinal virtues, which point toward the divine decad of the soul and also comprise the other blessed decad of the ten commandments. For [425] the tetrad is the decad in power, which is composed of the monad in sequence by progression. And again the same monad monadically contains the good by integration and demonstrates that the simple and that which is without parts of the divine activity is divided indivisibly from itself. By these decads, the soul strains itself to keep [430] the good which is proper to it unharmed, on the one hand, and on the other it courageously drives away that which is foreign [to the soul] as evil. This is so because, by these decads, the soul possesses a rational mind, a prudent wisdom, a practical contemplation, a virtuous knowledge, and the most faithful and unchanging "ceaseless knowledge,"[92] and because the soul brings the effects to their causes and the activities to the powers which have been joined to [435] God by prudence, and she receives in return for these theosis, which produces simplicity.

---

[91]ἡνίκα; the term is correlative with τηνικαῦτα ("then") in the following sentence. Maximus is clear that all of the following are conditions of the soul's union with God.

[92]The soul has a defensive and an offensive role in the preservation of its good because the soul has active and contemplative parts.

Ἐνέργεια γάρ ἐστι καὶ φανέρωσις τοῦ μὲν νοῦ ὁ λόγος ὡς αἰτίας αἰτιατόν· καὶ τῆς σοφίας ἡ φρόνησις, καὶ τῆς θεωρίας ἡ πρᾶξις, καὶ τῆς γνώσεως ἡ ἀρετή, καὶ τῆς ἀλήστου γνώσεως ἡ πίστις· ἐξ ὧν ἡ ἐνδιάθετος πρός τε τὴν ἀλήθειαν καὶ τὸ ἀγαθόν, φημὶ δὲ⁵¹ τὸν Θεόν, σχέσις δημιουργεῖται, ἣν ἔφασκεν εἶναι θείαν ἐπιστήμην καὶ <680c> γνῶσιν ἄπταιστον καὶ ἀγάπην καὶ εἰρήνην, ἐν αἷς καὶ δι' ὧν ἡ θέωσις· τὴν μὲν [ἐπιστήμην]⁵² ὡς συμπλήρωσιν πάσης τῆς ἐφικτῆς ἀνθρώποις περὶ Θεοῦ καὶ τῶν θείων γνώσεως καὶ τῶν ἀρετῶν περιοχὴν ἄπταιστον,⁵³ τὴν δὲ γνώμην⁵⁴ ὡς ἐπιβᾶσαν γνησίως τῇ ἀληθείᾳ, καὶ πεῖραν τοῦ θείου διαρκῆ παρεχομένην, τὴν δὲ [ἀγάπην]⁵⁵ ὡς ὅλης τοῦ Θεοῦ κατὰ διάθεσιν ὅλην μετέχουσαν τῆς τερπνότητος, τὴν δὲ [εἰρήνην]⁵⁶ ὡς τὰ αὐτὰ τῷ Θεῷ πάσχουσαν καὶ πάσχειν τοὺς κατ' αὐτὴν ἀξιωθέντας γενέσθαι παρασκευάζουσαν.

Εἰ γὰρ τὸ θεῖον παντελῶς ἀκίνητον, ὡς τὸ διοχλοῦν καθ' ὁτιοῦν οὐκ ἔχον (τί γὰρ καὶ τὸ φθάνον ἐστὶ τὴν ἐκείνου περιωπήν;) τῇ⁵⁷ δὲ εἰρήνη σταθερότης ἐστὶν ἀκλόνητός τε καὶ ἀκίνητος· πρὸς δέ, καὶ ἀνενόχλητος εὐφροσύνη· ἆρα τὰ θεῖα οὐ⁵⁸ πάσχει καὶ <680d> πᾶσα ψυχή, ἡ τὴν θείαν καταξιωθεῖσα κομίσασθαι εἰρήνην; ὡς μὴ μόνον κακίας καὶ ἀγνωσίας, ψεύδους τε καὶ πονηρίας, τῶν τε⁵⁹ ἀρετῇ καὶ⁶⁰ γνώσει, τῇ τε ἀληθείᾳ καὶ τῷ ἀγαθῷ ἀντικειμένων κακιῶν, αἳ ταῖς παρὰ φύσιν τῆς ψυχῆς κινήσεσι παρυφίστανται, ἀλλ' ἤδη καὶ ἀρετῆς⁶¹ καὶ γνώσεως, ἀληθείας τε αὖ καὶ ἀγαθότητος τῶν ἡμῖν διεγνωσμένων τοὺς ὅρους, εἰ θέμις εἰπεῖν, ὑπερβᾶσα,

---

⁵¹δὴ CCSG
⁵²om. CCSG
⁵³om. CCSG
⁵⁴om. CCSG
⁵⁵om. CCSG
⁵⁶om. CCSG
⁵⁷ἡ CCSG
⁵⁸om. CCSG
⁵⁹τῇ CCSG
⁶⁰καὶ τῇ CCSG
⁶¹ἀρετῆς αὐτῆς CCSG

For reason is indeed an activity and manifestation of the mind— [CCSG 28] as an effect is of a cause—and prudence of wisdom, and practice of contemplation, and virtue of knowledge, and faith of "ceaseless [440] knowledge." And from these the inner relationship with the true and the good (I am speaking about God) is fashioned, and the blessed elder said that this inner relationship is divine expertise and infallible knowledge and love and peace—in which and through which is theosis. It is divine expertise because it is the fulfillment of all knowledge that is possible for men concerning God and divine things and the content of the virtues. It is infallible knowledge because it [445] genuinely enters into the truth and produces a lasting experience of the divine. It is love because it partakes completely in the complete delight of God by disposition. It is peace because it suffers the same things as God and prepares those who are worthy to suffer to live according to peace.

For if the divine is completely immovable because it does not [CCSG 29; have anything that disturbs it (for what can attain to the contempla- [450]] tion of the divine?), and if peace is unshaken and immovable steadiness, and, additionally, undisturbed gladness, then every soul[93] "experiences divine things"[94] when it is deemed worthy to bring divine peace. The soul experiences the divine things because, if it [455] is right to speak so, it transcends the boundaries not only of what we determine to be wickedness and ignorance, falsehood and evil, the wicked things that resist virtue and knowledge, truth and the good, and that stand alongside the movements of the soul that are contrary to nature, but it also transcends the boundaries of its own [460] virtue and knowledge, truth and goodness. The soul quiets[95] itself in an ineffable and unknowable fashion for an intercourse with God

[93]ψυχή ("soul") and corresponding personal pronouns are feminine in Greek. Maximus portrays the soul as feminine in the sexual metaphor that he develops below.

[94]Pseudo-Dionysius, *On the Divine Names* 2.9.

[95]The verb "quiets" is syntactically parallel to the verb "transcends" above. Thus, Maximus is saying: "The soul experiences the divine things because it transcends . . . and because it quiets itself. . . ."

καὶ τῇ ὑπεραληθεστάτῃ καὶ ὑπεραγάθῳ κοίτῃ τοῦ Θεοῦ κατὰ τὴν ἀψευδεστάτην αὐτοῦ ἐπαγγελίαν ἀρρήτως τε καὶ ἀγνώστως ἑαυτὴν κατευνάσασα, ὡς μηδὲν τῶν διοχλεῖν αὐτῇ πεφυκότων λοιπὸν ἔχουσα φθάνον αὐτῆς τὴν ἐν Θεῷ κρυφιότητα· καθ᾽ ἣν μακαρίαν καὶ παναγίαν <681a> κοίτην τὸ φρικτὸν ἐκεῖνο τῆς ὑπὲρ νοῦν καὶ λόγον ἑνότητος μυστήριον ἐπιτελεῖται, δι᾽ οὗ μία σὰρξ καὶ ἓν πνεῦμα, ὅ τε Θεὸς πρὸς τὴν Ἐκκλησίαν, τὴν[62] ψυχήν, καὶ ἡ ψυχὴ πρὸς τὸν Θεὸν γενήσεται· ὦ πῶς σε Χριστέ, θαυμάσω τῆς ἀγαθότητος, οὐ γὰρ ἀμυνῆσαι φάναι τολμήσω, ὁ μήτε πρὸς τὸ θαυμάζειν ἀξίως ἀρκοῦσαν ἔχων τὴν δύναμιν· Ἔσονται γὰρ οἱ δύο εἰς σάρκα μίαν· τὸ δὲ μυστήριον τοῦτο μέγα ἐστίν· ἐγὼ δὲ λέγω εἰς Χριστὸν καὶ τὴν Ἐκκλησίαν, φησὶν ὁ θεῖος Ἀπόστολος. καὶ πάλιν· Ὁ κολλώμενος τῷ Κυρίῳ, ἓν πνεῦμά ἐστι.

<681b> Οὕτω γοῦν ἐνοειδῆ γενομένην ψυχὴν[63] καὶ πρὸς ἑαυτὴν καὶ Θεῷ[64] συναχθεῖσαν οὐκ ἔσται ὁ εἰς πολλὰ κατ᾽ ἐπίνοιαν αὐτὴν ἔτι διαιρῶν λόγος, τῷ πρώτῳ καὶ μόνῳ καὶ ἑνὶ Λόγῳ τε καὶ Θεῷ κατεστεμμένην τὴν κεφαλήν· ἐν ᾧ κατὰ μίαν ἀπερινόητον ἁπλότητα πάντες οἱ τῶν ὄντων λόγοι ἑνοειδῶς καὶ εἰσὶ καὶ ὑφεστήκασιν, ὡς δημιουργῷ τῶν ὄντων καὶ ποιητῇ· ᾧ ἐνατενίζουσα οὐκ ἐκτὸς αὐτῆς ὄντι, ἀλλ᾽ ἐν ὅλῃ ὅλῳ, κατὰ ἁπλῆν προσβολὴν εἴσεται καὶ αὐτὴ τοὺς τῶν ὄντων λόγους καὶ τὰς αἰτίας, δι᾽ οὓς τυχὸν πρὶν νυμφευθῆναι τῷ Λόγῳ καὶ Θεῷ ταῖς διαιρετικαῖς ὑπήγετο μεθόδοις, σωστικῶς τε δι᾽ αὐτῶν καὶ ἐναρμονίως πρὸς

---

[62]om. CCSG
[63]τὴν ψυχὴν CCSG
[64]τὸν θεὸν CCSG

that is absolutely beyond truth and beyond good and that he offered us according to his most trustworthy promise. For at last there is not anything that by nature disturbs it and enters its hiddenness in God. It is there that the awe-inspiring mystery of the unity that is beyond mind and reason, the blessed and all-holy intercourse, is [465] celebrated[96]—the mystery through which God will become "one flesh"[97] and "one spirit"[98] with[99] the Church (that is, the soul), and the soul with God. How I will worship you for your goodness, O [CCSG 30] Christ! But, I will not dare to sing praises or speak, I who do not have [470] sufficient ability to worship you in a worthy manner. For "the two shall become one flesh. And this mystery is great, and I am saying that it refers to Christ and the Church,"[100] says the divine Apostle. And again: "But he who is united to the Lord becomes one spirit with him."[101]

So then, because the soul "becomes one"[102] in this fashion and is brought together to itself and to God, there will be no reason to fur- [475] ther divide the soul conceptually into many parts; the soul has been crowned as the head by the first, only, and one God the Word.[103] All the principles of everything that exists are and subsist singly in him according to one unintelligible simplicity, since he is the creator and maker of everything that exists. Looking intently on him who is not [480] outside the soul but the whole in the whole soul,[104] even the soul by this simple contact will see into the principles and the causes of the things that exist. Before the soul was wedded to God the Word, it was led into divisive pursuits perhaps by the principles and causes, but it is now being brought salvifically and harmoniously even

[96]ἐπιτελέω; this term can mean to celebrate the Eucharist.

[97]1 Cor 6.16 (cf. Gen 2.24).

[98]1 Cor 6.17.

[99]πρός; this is the same preposition by which the Apostle John affirms that the Word was "with" God (Jn 1.1).

[100]Eph 5.31–32.

[101]1 Cor 6.17.

[102]Pseudo-Dionysius, *On the Divine Names* 4.9.

[103]Lit. "the God Word" (likewise for every instance of "God the Word" below).

[104]In other words, it is God who gives unity and coherence to the soul's being.

αὐτὸν φερομένῃ, τὸν παντὸς λόγου καὶ πάσης αἰτίας περιεκτικόν
τε καὶ ποιητήν.

<681c> Ἐπειδὴ ταῦτα τοίνυν τῆς ψυχῆς εἰσιν, ὡς ἔφαμεν, κατὰ
νοῦν μὲν ἐχούσης δυνάμει τὴν σοφίαν, ἐκ δὲ τῆς σοφίας τὴν
θεωρίαν, ἐκ δὲ ταύτης τὴν γνῶσιν, ἐκ δὲ τῆς γνώσεως τὴν ἄληστον
γνῶσιν, δι' ἧς πρὸς τὴν ἀλήθειαν ὡς πέρας καὶ τέλος οὖσαν
τῶν κατὰ νοῦν ἀγαθῶν ἄγεται· κατὰ δὲ τὸν λόγον ἐχούσης
τὴν φρόνησιν, ἐκ δὲ ταύτης τὴν πρᾶξιν, ἐκ δὲ τῆς πράξεως τὴν
ἀρετήν, ἐκ δὲ ταύτης τὴν πίστιν, καθ' ἣν εἰς τὸ ἀγαθὸν ὡς
τέλος μακάριον τῶν λογικῶν ἐνεργιῶν καταλήγει· δι' ὧν ἡ τῶν
θείων ἐπιστήμη κατὰ σύνοδον τῆς πρὸς ἄλληλα τούτων ἑνώσεως
συλλέγεται. πρὸς ταῦτα πάντα σαφῶς ἁρμόζεται,⁶⁵ κατὰ τὴν
θεωρίαν εἰκαζομένη τῇ ψυχῇ ἡ ἁγία τοῦ Θεοῦ Ἐκκλησία. τὰ
μὲν κατὰ νοῦν πάντα καὶ <681d> ἐκ τοῦ νοῦ κατὰ πρόοδον εἶναι
δειχθέντα διὰ τοῦ ἱερατείου σημαίνουσα, τὰ δὲ κατὰ τὸν λόγον
καὶ ἐκ τοῦ λόγου κατὰ διαστολὴν εἶναι δηλωθέντα διὰ τοῦ ναοῦ
σαφηνίζουσα, καὶ πάντα συνάγουσα πρὸς τὸ τελούμενον ἐπὶ τοῦ
θείου θυσιαστηρίου μυστήριον· ὅπερ διὰ τῶν κατὰ τὴν Ἐκκλησίαν
ἐπιτελουμένων ὁ δυνηθεὶς ἐμφρόνως⁶⁶ καὶ σοφῶς μυηθῆναι,
Ἐκκλησίαν ὄντως Θεοῦ, καὶ θείαν τὴν ἑαυτοῦ ψυχὴν κατεστήσατο·
δι' ἣν ἴσως καὶ ἧς ἡ χειροποίητος Ἐκκλησία σοφῶς διὰ τῆς ἐν αὐτῇ
τῶν θείων ποικιλίας <684a> κατὰ σύμβολον οὖσα παράδειγμα πρὸς
ὁδηγίαν τοῦ κρείττονος ἡμῖν παρεδόθη.

---

⁶⁵ἁρμόσεται CCSG
⁶⁶ἐμφρόνως τε CCSG

through them to him, the one who is the maker of and encompasses every principle and every cause.   [485]

Therefore, since these things are proper to the soul, as we said above, on the one hand, according to the mind, the soul possesses wisdom in power, and from wisdom contemplation, and from this, knowledge, and from knowledge "ceaseless knowledge," through which the soul is led to the truth, which exists as the limit and end of the good things according to the mind. But on the other hand, [CCSG 31' according to reason, the soul possesses prudence, and from this, [490] practice, and from practice virtue, and from this, faith, according to which the soul ends in the good as the blessed end of the rational activities. Through these activities, expertise in divine things is gathered by integration from the oneness of all[105] of these things with one another. The holy Church of God, which is imaged by the soul, will [495] be seen to correspond clearly with all these things in contemplation; on the one hand, the Church signifies through the sanctuary everything that has been demonstrated to exist by progression according to the mind and from the mind; and on the other hand, the Church articulates through the nave the things that have been revealed to exist by precept according to reason and from reason.[106] The Church [500] brings together all things to the mystery performed on the divine altar. And, therefore, the one who is able to be initiated in prudence and wisdom through the rites that are celebrated in the Church [establishes his very soul as a Church truly of God and divine. The Church made by hands has been built in wisdom for the soul and [505] also as a symbolic model of the soul through the Church's various divine rites; it was given to us as a guide to that which is better.

[105]We added in "all" to the English text in order to note that Maximus is referring here to the decad.

[106]At the beginning of chapter 5, Maximus divided the decad into two parts, representing the mind and reason as two parts of the soul. He returns to this paradigm now: the sanctuary (i.e., the part of the Church that corresponds to the mind of the soul) is the place where the people are exhorted to live according to virtue and where one progresses in the virtues; the nave (i.e., the part of the Church that corresponds to the reason of the soul) is the place where the commandments are delivered and where one learns the precepts.

Κεφαλ. S. Πῶς καὶ ποίῳ τρόπῳ ἄνθρωπος λέγεται καὶ ἡ ἁγία Γραφή

Ὥσπερ δὲ τῇ κατὰ ἀναγωγὴν θεωρίᾳ τὴν Ἐκκλησίαν ἔλεγεν ἄνθρωπον εἶναι πνευματικόν, μυστικὴν δὲ Ἐκκλησίαν τὸν ἄνθρωπον, οὕτω δὴ καὶ τὴν ἁγίαν πᾶσαν κατὰ συναίρεσιν Γραφήν, ἄνθρωπον ἔφασκεν εἶναι, τὴν μὲν Παλαιὰν Διαθήκην ἔχουσαν σῶμα, ψυχὴν δὲ καὶ πνεῦμα καὶ νοῦν τὴν Καινήν. καὶ <684b> πάλιν ὅλης τῆς ἁγίας Γραφῆς, Παλαιᾶς τέ φημι καὶ Νέας, τὸ καθ᾽ ἱστορίαν γράμμα, σῶμα· τὸν δὲ νοῦν τῶν γεγραμμένων καὶ τὸν σκοπόν, πρὸς ὃν ὁ νοῦς ἀποτέτακται,[67] ψυχήν. Ὅπερ ἀκούσας ἐγώ,[68] μάλιστα τῆς εἰκασίας ἠγάσθην τὸ ἀκριβές, καὶ τὸν κατ᾽ ἀξίαν ἑκάστῳ διανέμοντα χαρίσματα δεόντως ἀνύμνησα κατὰ δύναμιν. ὡς γὰρ θνητὸς ὁ καθ᾽ ἡμᾶς ἄνθρωπος κατὰ τὸ φαινόμενον, κατὰ δὲ τὸ μὴ φαινόμενον ἀθάνατος, οὕτω καὶ ἡ ἁγία Γραφή, τὸ μὲν φαινόμενον γράμμα παρερχόμενον ἔχουσα, τὸ δὲ κρυπτόμενον τῷ γράμματι πνεῦμα μηδέποτε τοῦ εἶναι παυόμενον ἀληθῆ τὸν λόγον τῆς θεωρίας συνίστησι. καὶ ὥσπερ οὗτος ὁ καθ᾽ ἡμᾶς ἄνθρωπος, φιλοσοφίᾳ κρατῶν τῆς ἐμπαθοῦς ὀρέξεώς τε καὶ ὁρμῆς <684c> μαραίνει τὴν σάρκα, οὕτω καὶ ἡ ἁγία Γραφὴ νοουμένη πνευματικῶς τὸ γράμμα ἑαυτῆς περιτέμνει. φησὶ γὰρ ὁ θεῖος[69] Ἀπόστολος· ὅσον ὁ ἔξω ἡμῶν ἄνθρωπος διαφθείρεται, τοσοῦτον ὁ ἔσω ἀνακαινοῦται ἡμέρα καὶ ἡμέρα. τοῦτο νοείσθω καὶ λεγέσθω καὶ ἐπὶ τῆς ἁγίας Γραφῆς, ἀνθρώπου τροπικῶς νοουμένης. Ὅσον γὰρ αὐτῆς τὸ γράμμα ὑποχωρεῖ, τοσοῦτον τὸ πνεῦμα πλεονεκτεῖ·

---

[67] ἀποτέταται CCSG
[68] ἔγωγε CCSG
[69] μέγας CCSG

(6) How and in What Mode the Holy Scripture also Is Said to Be a Human Being

And as the blessed elder said in sublime contemplation that the Church is a spiritual human being and that a human being is a mystical Church, in similar fashion he stated that all holy Scripture in its entirety is a human being: The Old Testament possesses a body, and the New possesses a soul and spirit and mind. And, again, the historical letter[107] of all holy Scripture (I am speaking of the Old and the New Testaments) is the body. And the mind of the Scripture and the aim towards which it refers is the soul.[108] And when I learned this, I very much admired the exactness of the comparison, and I ascribed due praise to the best of my ability to the one who distributes gifts to each one according to his worth.[109] For, as "the human being in our nature"[110] is mortal in that which is seen but immortal in that which is not seen, so also the holy Scripture—which possesses a letter that passes away[111] in that which is seen and a spirit that never ceases to exist in that which is hidden in the letter—establishes the true word of contemplation. And as this "man in our nature" by controlling the urges and impulses of the passions through philosophy lets the flesh wither away, so also the holy Scripture, when perceived spiritually, circumcises its letter. For the great apostle says: To the extent that "our outer nature is wasting away," so "our inner nature is being renewed every day."[112] Let this be perceived and said concerning the holy Scripture, when it is perceived figuratively to be a human being. For to the extent that its "letter withdraws" so "the spirit advances"[113]

[CCSG 32]
[510]

[515]

[520]

[525]

---

[107]τὸ καθ' ἱστορίαν γράμμα; this phrase could also be translated: "the literal reading of the text."

[108]Cf. Phil 4.13–14.

[109]Cf. Rom 12.6.

[110]Gregory Nazianzus, *Oration* 30.12.

[111]παρέρχομαι; it is unfortunate that word here translated "to pass away" is precisely the same word as in Matthew 24.35 where Jesus says that his word shall never pass away.

[112]2 Cor 4.16; the word translated twice in this sentence as "nature" is literally "human being" (ἄνθρωπος).

[113]Gregory of Nazianzus, *Oration* 38.2 (trans. Harrison, p. 61).

καὶ ὅσον αἱ σκιαὶ τῆς προσκαίρου λατρείας παρατρέχουσι, τοσοῦτον ἡ ἀλήθεια τῆς πίστεως ἡ παμφαής τε καὶ ὁλολαμπὴς καὶ ἄσκιος ἐπεισέρχεται, καθ᾽ ἣν καὶ δι᾽ ἣν προηγουμένως καὶ ἔστι καὶ γέγραπται καὶ Γραφὴ λέγεται, τῷ νῷ διὰ χάριτος πνευματικῆς ἐγχαραττομένη, ὥσπερ καὶ ὁ καθ᾽ ἡμᾶς ἄνθρωπος διὰ τὴν ψυχὴν τὴν λογικήν τε καὶ νοερὰν προηγουμένως <684d> ἄνθρωπος μάλιστα καὶ ἔστι καὶ λέγεται· καθ᾽ ἣν καὶ δι᾽ ἣν εἰκών τε καὶ ὁμοίωσίς ἐστι Θεοῦ τοῦ ποιήσαντος αὐτὸν καὶ τῶν λοιπῶν ζώων φυσικῶς ἀποδιώρισται, μηδεμίαν πρὸς αὐτὰ σχετικῆς δυνάμεως τὴν οἱανοῦν ἔμφασιν ἔχων.

Κεφαλ. Ζ. Πῶς ὁ κόσμος ἄνθρωπος λέγεται· καὶ ποίῳ τρόπῳ καὶ ὁ ἄνθρωπος, κόσμος

Κατὰ ταύτην δὲ πάλιν εὐμιμήτως τὴν εἰκόνα καὶ τὸν κόσμον ὅλον τὸν ἐξ ὁρατῶν καὶ ἀοράτων συνιστάμενον, <685a> ἄνθρωπον ὑπέβαλλεν εἶναι· καὶ κόσμον αὖθις τὸν ἐκ ψυχῆς καὶ σώματος, ἄνθρωπον· ψυχῆς γὰρ λόγον ἐπέχειν ἔλεγε τὰ νοητά, ὥσπερ καὶ ἡ ψυχὴ τῶν νοητῶν· καὶ σώματος τύπον[70] ἐπέχειν τὰ αἰσθητά, ὥσπερ καὶ τῶν αἰσθητῶν τὸ σῶμα. καὶ ψυχὴν μὲν εἶναι τῶν αἰσθητῶν τὰ νοητά, σῶμα δὲ τῶν νοητῶν τὰ αἰσθητά. καὶ ὡς ψυχὴν ἐνοῦσαν σώματι, τῷ αἰσθητῷ κόσμῳ τὸν νοητὸν εἶναι· καὶ[71] τῷ νοητῷ τὸν αἰσθητόν, ὡς σῶμα τῇ ψυχῇ συγκροτούμενον· καὶ ἕνα ἐξ ἀμφοῖν εἶναι κόσμον, ὥσπερ καὶ ἐκ ψυχῆς καὶ σώματος ἄνθρωπον ἕνα, μηδ᾽ ἑτέρου τούτων τῶν ἀλλήλοις καθ᾽ ἕνωσιν συμπεφυκότων θάτερον ἀρνουμένου καὶ ἀποπέμποντος, διὰ τὸν τοῦ συνδήσαντος νόμον, καθ᾽ ὃν τῆς ἑνοποιοῦ δυνάμεως ὁ λόγος ἐνέσπαρται μὴ συγχωρῶν τὴν καθ᾽ <685b> ὑπόστασιν ἐπὶ τῇ ἑνώσει

---

[70]τόπον CCSG
[71]om. CCSG

and to the extent that "the shadows" of temporal worship "flee away," [530]
so the all-shining, all-radiant, and shadowless "truth"[114] of the faith [CCSG 33]
"streams in." According to and on account of this truth, Scripture
in its essence is and is written and is said to be Scripture when it
is engraved in the mind through spiritual grace, as also certainly
"a human being in his nature" in essence is and is called man on
account of the rational and intelligible soul. According to and on
account of the soul, the human being is the "image" and "likeness of
God"[115] who made him, and he is separated from the rest of the ani- [535]
mals by nature because he possesses the reflection of the relational
power in a completely different way than they do.[116]

(7) How the Universe is Called a Human Being and in What Mode a Human Being is Called the Universe

And again, according to the very helpful image, the blessed elder[117] [540]
submitted that the whole universe (which is composed of visible and
invisible things) is a human being, and again, that a human being
(who is composed of the soul and body) is the universe. He said that
the intelligible things present the reason of the soul, even as the soul
presents the reason of the intelligible things, and that the sensible
things present the place of the body, even as the body presents the [545]
place of the sensible things. The intelligible things are the soul of the
sensible things, and the sensible things are the body of the intelligible
things. And as the soul dwells in the body, so that which is intelligible [CCSG 34]
exists in the sensible realm; and that which is sensible exists in the
intelligible, as the body is held together by the soul. He said that
the one universe is composed of both realms,[118] just as one man is
composed of soul and body. Neither of these things, which are one [550]
with one another by nature, denies or divorces the other on account

[114]Ibid.

[115]Gen 1.26.

[116]I.e., the way that man reflects God is completely different from the way that the animals reflect God.

[117]"Blessed elder" is not specifically stated in the Greek text.

[118]I.e., the intelligible and sensible realms.

ταυτότητα τούτων ἀγνοηθῆναι, διὰ τὴν φυσικὴν ἑτερότητα, μηδ᾽ εἶναι δυνατωτέραν πρὸς διάστασίν τε καὶ μερισμὸν τὴν ἕκαστον τούτων ἑαυτῷ περιγράφουσαν ἰδιότητα τῆς μυστικῶς καθ᾽ ἕνωσιν αὐτοῖς ἐντεθείσης φιλικῆς συγγενείας ἀποφανθῆναι, καθ᾽ ἣν ὁ καθ᾽ ὅλου καὶ εἷς τρόπος τῆς ἐν ὅλοις ἀφανοῦς καὶ ἀγνώστου παρουσίας τῆς τῶν ὄντων συνεκτικῆς αἰτίας ποικίλως πᾶσιν ἐνυπάρχων καὶ καθ᾽ ἑαυτὰ καὶ ἐν ἀλλήλοις τὰ ὅλα συνίστησιν ἄφυρτα καὶ ἀδιαίρετα· καὶ ἀλλήλων μᾶλλον ἢ ἑαυτῶν κατὰ τὴν ἑνοποιὸν σχέσιν ὄντα παρίστησι, μέχρις οὗ λῦσαι παραστῇ τῷ συνδήσαντι μείζονος ἕνεκα καὶ μυστικωτέρας οἰκονομίας κατὰ τὸν καιρὸν τῆς ἐλπιζομένης καθολικῆς συντελείας, καθ᾽ ἣν καὶ ὁ κόσμος, ὡς ἄνθρωπος, τῶν <685c> φαινομένων⁷² τεθνήξεται, καὶ πάλιν ἀναστήσεται νέος ἐκ γεγηρακότος, κατὰ τὴν παραυτίκα προσδοκωμένην ἀνάστασιν· ἡνίκα καὶ ὁ καθ᾽ ἡμᾶς ἄνθρωπος, ὡς μέρος τῷ ὅλῳ καὶ μικρὸς τῷ μεγάλῳ, συναναστήσεται κόσμῳ, τὴν πρὸς τὸ μηκέτι δύνασθαι φθείρεσθαι κομισάμενος δύναμιν, ὅταν ἐμφερῆ τῇ τε ψυχῇ τὸ σῶμα καὶ τοῖς νοητοῖς τὰ αἰσθητὰ κατ᾽ εὐπρέπειαν καὶ δόξαν γενήσεται, μιᾶς ὅλοις κατ᾽ ἐναργῆ τε καὶ ἐνεργὸν παρουσίαν ἀναλόγως ἑκάστῳ θείας ἐπιφαινομένης δυνάμεως, καὶ δι᾽ ἑαυτῆς τὸν τῆς ἑνώσεως ἄλυτον εἰς τοὺς ἀπείρους αἰῶνας συντηρούσης δεσμόν.

<685d> Εἴ τις οὖν βούλεται καὶ βίον καὶ λόγον θεοφιλῆ καὶ θεάρεστον ἔχειν, τῶν τριῶν τούτων ἀνθρώπων—τοῦ κόσμου τέ φημι, καὶ τῆς ἁγίας Γραφῆς, καὶ τοῦ καθ᾽ ἡμᾶς—τὰ κρείττω

---

⁷²τῶν φαινομένων : τῷ φαινομένῳ CCSG

of the law of him who bound them together. It is according to this law that the reason of the uniting power is implanted, but this reason does not permit the identity of substance in their oneness to be mis-understood because of their diversity by nature.[119] For the particu- [555] larities that limit each of these things in itself and tend to separation and division is shown not to be stronger than the amicable affinity that was mystically engrafted into them and is inclined to oneness. It is according to this affinity that the universal and singular mode of the invisible and unknowable presence of the cause that holds [560] all things together in both realms subsists in everything variously, and it unites all things in themselves and to one another, and they become unmixed and undivided. And it renders them as belonging to one another rather than to themselves according to the uniting relationship until such time as "he who bound it together sees fit to undo it"[120] on account of the greater and more mystical dispensa-tion at the time of the universal consummation for which we hope. [565] The universe, as a man, will then have perished in that which can be [CCSG 35] seen, and it will be raised again—new from that which has grown old—at the resurrection that we presently await. "The human being in his human nature,"[121] as a part of the whole and a portion of the totality, will then be raised together with the universe, and he will recover the power no longer to be able to be corrupted. The body [570] will resemble the soul and the sensible things the intelligible things in dignity and glory, when the one divine power will be revealed in everything by its manifest and effective presence commensurately revealed in each one, and it is this very power that will preserve the [575] indestructible bond of oneness forever and ever.

If, therefore, someone wishes to have God-loving and God-pleasing life and speech, let him do the best and most honorable things of these three men—I am speaking about the universe and

---

[119]While it bonds the sensible and intelligible realms together in the universe as we experience it, still reason does not obscure these two realms such that our minds fail to perceive them as distinct parts of reality.

[120]Gregory of Nazianzus, *Oration* 32.8 (trans. Vinson, p. 197).

[121]Gregory Nazianzus, *Oration* 30.12.

περὶ πολλοῦ ποιείτω καὶ τιμιώτερα. ψυχῆς[73] μὲν ὅση δύναμις ἐπιμελείσθω[74] τῆς ἀθανάτου καὶ θείας καὶ θεοποιηθησομένης ἐξ ἀρετῶν, καὶ σαρκὸς καταφρονείτω τῆς ὑποκειμένης φθορᾷ καὶ θανάτῳ καὶ τὸ τῆς ψυχῆς ἀμελούμενον <688a> ῥυπῶσαι δυναμένης ἀξίωμα. φθαρτὸν γὰρ σῶμα, φησί, βαρύνει ψυχήν, καὶ βρίθει τὸ γεῶδες σκῆνος νοῦν πολυφρόντιδα. καὶ πάλιν· ἡ σὰρξ ἐπιθυμεῖ κατὰ τοῦ πνεύματος· τὸ δὲ πνεῦμα κατὰ τῆς σαρκός. καὶ αὖθις· ὁ σπείρων εἰς τὴν σάρκα ἑαυτοῦ, ἐκ τῆς σαρκὸς θερίσει φθοράν. πρὸς δὲ τὰς ἀσωμάτους καὶ νοερὰς δυνάμεις κατὰ νοῦν διὰ νοήσεως κινησάτω τὴν ἅμιλλαν, ἀφεὶς τὰ παρόντα καὶ βλεπόμενα· τὰ γὰρ βλεπόμενα πρόσκαιρα, φησί, τὰ δὲ μὴ βλεπόμενα, αἰώνια· αἷς διὰ τὸ πλῆθος τῆς κατ᾽ εἰρήνην ἕξεως ὁ Θεὸς ἐναναπαύεται. καὶ πρὸς τὸ Πνεῦμα τὸ ἅγιον δι᾽ ἔμφρονος μελέτης τῆς ἁγίας Γραφῆς ὑπερβὰς τὸ γράμμα σωφρόνως ἀναφερέσθω· ἐν ᾧ τὸ πλήρωμα ὑπάρχει τῶν ἀγαθῶν καὶ οἱ θησαυροὶ τῆς γνώσεως καὶ τῆς σοφίας <688b> ἀπόκρυφοι, ὧν εἴ τις ἐντὸς ἄξιος γενέσθαι φανήσεται τὸν Θεὸν αὐτὸν εὑρήσει ταῖς πλαξὶ τῆς καρδίας ἐγγεγραμμένον διὰ τῆς ἐν πνεύματι χάριτος, ἀνακεκαλυμμένῳ προσώπῳ τὴν τοῦ Θεοῦ δόξαν ἐνοπτριζόμενος τῇ περιαιρέσει τοῦ κατὰ γράμμα καλύμματος.

Κεφαλ. Η. Τίνων εἰσὶ σύμβολα ἥ τε πρώτη τῆς ἁγίας συνάξεως εἴσοδος καὶ τὰ μετ᾽ αὐτὴν τελούμενα

Ἥκει δὲ λοιπὸν ὁ λόγος ἡμῖν κατὰ τὴν σύντομον ἔκθεσιν τῶν εἰρημένων περὶ τῆς ἁγίας Ἐκκλησίας θεωριῶν παρὰ τοῦ μακαρίου

---

[73]καὶ ψυχῆς CCSG
[74]ἐπιμελείτω CCSG

holy Scripture and "the human being in his human nature."[122] Let him take care of his soul to the best of his ability, for it is immortal, divine, and will be deified through the virtues; but let him despise [580] the flesh, which lies in corruption and death and is able to defile the dignity of the soul when it is neglected. "For a corruptible body burdens the soul, and the earthly tent weighs down a mind full of cares."[123] And again, "The flesh lusts against the Spirit, and the Spirit [585] against the flesh."[124] And once more, "The one who sows to his own flesh will from the flesh reap corruption."[125] Let him move the conflict to the bodiless and intellectual powers according to the mind [CCSG 36] through knowledge, leaving behind the things that are present and seen. "For the things that are seen are transient, but the things that [590] are unseen are eternal."[126] God rests in these powers on account of the greatness of their habit resulting in peace. And by going beyond the letter of the holy Scripture through prudent study, let him in prudence raise himself up to the Holy Spirit, in whom exists the fullness of good things and in whom "are hid the treasures of knowledge and wisdom."[127] If anyone is shown to be inwardly worthy of these [595] treasures, he will find that God himself has been inscribed on the "tablets of the heart" through grace in the Spirit, and he will "behold the glory"[128] of God "with unveiled face" by the "removal of the veil" of the letter.

(8) What is the Symbolism of the First Entrance of the Holy Synaxis and that which is Performed Thereafter

Now that we have concluded our concise exposition of the contem- [600] plations of the blessed elder concerning the holy Church, we will do

[122]Ibid.
[123]Wis 9.15.
[124]Gal 5.17.
[125]Gal 6.8.
[126]2 Cor 4.18.
[127]Col 2.3. It is noteworthy that Maximus applies this statement to the Holy Spirit, which is about Christ in its original context.
[128]2 Cor 3.18; cf. Ex 34.34.

γέροντος, συντομωτέραν καὶ τὴν περὶ τῆς ἁγίας τῆς Ἐκκλησίας[75] συνάξεως <688c> διήγησιν, ὡς οἷόν τε, ποιησόμενος.

Τὴν μὲν οὖν πρώτην εἰς τὴν ἁγίαν Ἐκκλησίαν τοῦ ἀρχιερέως κατὰ τὴν ἱερὰν σύναξιν εἴσοδον τῆς πρώτης τοῦ Υἱοῦ τοῦ Θεοῦ καὶ Σωτῆρος ἡμῶν Χριστοῦ διὰ σαρκὸς εἰς τὸν κόσμον τοῦτον παρουσίας τύπον καὶ εἰκόνα φέρειν ἐδίδασκε, δι' ἧς τὴν δουλωθεῖσαν τῇ φθορᾷ καὶ παθοῦσαν ὑφ' ἑαυτῆς τῷ θανάτῳ διὰ τῆς ἁμαρτίας καὶ βασιλευομένην τυραννικῶς ὑπὸ τοῦ διαβόλου τῶν ἀνθρώπων φύσιν ἐλευθερώσας τε καὶ λυτρωσάμενος[76] πᾶσαν τὴν ὑπὲρ αὐτῆς ὀφειλὴν ὡς ὑπεύθυνος ἀποδοὺς ὁ ἀνεύθυνος καὶ ἀναμάρτητος, πάλιν πρὸς τὴν ἐξ ἀρχῆς ἐπανήγαγε τῆς βασιλείας χάριν, ἑαυτὸν λύτρον ὑπὲρ ἡμῶν δοὺς καὶ ἀντάλλαγμα, καὶ τῶν ἡμετέρων φθοροποιῶν παθημάτων τὸ ζωοποιὸν αὐτοῦ πάθος ἀντιδούς, παιώνιον ἄκος καὶ <688d> παντὸς τοῦ κόσμου σωτήριον, μεθ' ἣν παρουσίαν, ἡ εἰς οὐρανοὺς αὐτοῦ καὶ τὸν ὑπερουράνιον θρόνον ἀνάβασίς τε καὶ ἀποκατάστασις συμβολικῶς τυποῦται, διὰ τῆς ἐν τῷ ἱερατείῳ τοῦ ἀρχιερέως εἰσόδου καὶ τῆς εἰς τὸν θρόνον τὸν ἱερατικὸν ἀναβάσεως.

Κεφαλ. Θ. Τίνος ἔχει δήλωσιν καὶ ἡ τοῦ λαοῦ εἰς τὴν ἁγίαν τοῦ Θεοῦ Ἐκκλησίαν εἴσοδος

Τὴν δὲ τοῦ λαοῦ σὺν τῷ ἱεράρχῃ γενομένην εἰς τὴν Ἐκκλησίαν εἴσοδον, τὴν ἐξ[77] ἀγνοίας καὶ πλάνης <689a> εἰς ἐπίγνωσιν Θεοῦ ἐπιστροφὴν τῶν ἀπίστων, καὶ τὴν ἀπὸ κακίας καὶ ἀγνωσίας εἰς

---

[75]om. CCSG
[76]λυτρωσάμενος καὶ CCSG
[77]ἐξ ἀπιστίας εἰς πίστον καὶ ἐξ CCSG

our best to present an even more concise interpretation of the holy synaxis.

Therefore, he explained that the first entrance of the high priest [CCSG 37] into the holy Church during the sacred synaxis bears the represen- [605] tation and image of the first coming of the Son of God, Christ our Savior, who came in the flesh into this world. During his coming he set free and ransomed human nature, which was enslaved to corruption, sold by itself to death through sin,[129] and tyrannically ruled by [610] the devil. And when the innocent and sinless one paid the entire debt for human nature as though guilty, he restored us again to the grace of the kingdom at the beginning,[130] giving "himself as a ransom and an exchange for us."[131] And, in return for our corrupting passions, he [615] bestows his life-giving passion as the healing remedy that is salvific for all the world. The ascension of Christ into the heavens and the restoration of his throne above the heavens, after his coming, are symbolically represented through the entrance of the high priest into the sanctuary and his ascension to the priestly throne.

(9) What is the Interpretation of the Entrance of the People into [CCSG 38] the Holy Church of God

The blessed elder said that the entrance of the people with the [620] high priest into the Church signifies the conversion of the faithless from unbelief to faith and from ignorance and error to the

[129]Cf. Rom 5.12.

[130]Maximus seems to be referring to God's rule at the creation as the "kingdom," and so we understand that Maximus is saying that we are restored to the state that Adam and Eve possessed prior to the fall.

[131]Gregory of Nazianzus, *Oration* 1.5 (trans. Harrison, p. 59). This citation comes at the conclusion of one of the clearest expositions of the doctrine of theosis in all of patristic literature: "Let us become like Christ, since Christ also became like us; let us become gods because of him, since he also because of us became human. He assumed what is worse that he might give what is better. He became poor that we through his poverty might become rich. He took the form of a slave, that we might regain freedom. He descended that we might be lifted up, he was tempted that we might be victorious, he was dishonored to glorify us, he died to save us, he ascended to draw to himself us who lay below the Fall of sin. Let us give everything, offer everything, to the one who gave himself as a ransom and an exchange for us."

ἀρετὴν καὶ γνῶσιν μετάθεσιν τῶν πιστῶν σημαίνειν, ὁ μακάριος ἔλεγε γέρων. οὐ γὰρ μόνον τὴν ἐπὶ τὸν ἀληθινὸν[78] Θεὸν ἐπιστροφὴν τῶν ἀπίστων ἡ εἰς τὴν Ἐκκλησίαν εἴσοδος παραδηλοῖ, ἀλλὰ καὶ ἑκάστου ἡμῶν τῶν πιστευόντων μέν, ἀθετούντων δὲ τὰς ἐντολὰς τοῦ Κυρίου δι᾽ ἀγωγῆς ἀκολάστου καὶ ἀσχήμονος βίου, τὴν διὰ μετανοίας διόρθωσιν. πᾶς γὰρ ἄνθρωπος, εἴτε φονεύς, εἴτε μοιχός, εἴτε κλέπτης, εἴτε ὑπερήφανος, εἴτε ἀλαζών, ἢ ὑβριστής, ἢ πλεονέκτης, ἢ φιλάργυρος, ἢ κατάλαλος, ἢ μνησίκακος, ἢ πρὸς θυμὸν καὶ ὀργὴν εὐάγωγος, ἢ λοίδορος, ἢ συκοφάντης, ἢ ψίθυρος, ἢ φθόνῳ εὐχείρωτος, ἢ μέθυσος καὶ ἁπλῶς, ἵνα μὴ πάντα τὰ ἐκ[79] κακίας εἴδη ἀπαριθμούμενος μηκύνω τὸν λόγον, ὅστις ὑφ᾽ οἱασδήποτε κακίας ἐνεχόμενος, <689b> ἐπὸν[80] τοῦ ἑκουσίως κατ᾽ ἐπιτήδευσιν ἐνέχεσθαι καὶ ἐνεργεῖν κατὰ πρόθεσιν, παύσοιτο καὶ μεταβαλοῖ τὸν βίον ἐπὶ τὸ κρεῖττον, τῆς κακίας τὴν ἀρετὴν ἀνθαιρούμενος, ὁ τοιοῦτος κυρίως τε καὶ ἀληθῶς Χριστῷ τῷ Θεῷ καὶ ἀρχιερεῖ νοείσθω τε καὶ λεγέσθω συνεισιέναι εἰς τὴν ἀρετήν, Ἐκκλησίαν τροπικῶς νοουμένην.

Κεφαλ. I. Τίνων εἰσὶ σύμβολον τὰ θεῖα ἀναγνώσματα

Τὰς δὲ θείας τῶν πανιέρων βίβλων ἀναγνώσεις, τὰς θείας καὶ μακαρίας τοῦ παναγίου Θεοῦ βουλήσεις τε καὶ βουλὰς ὑπεμφαίνειν ἔλεγεν ὁ διδάσκαλος, δι᾽ ὧν τὰς ὑποθήκας τῶν πρακτέων ἀναλόγως <689c> ἕκαστος ἡμῶν κατὰ τὴν ὑποῦσαν αὐτῷ δύναμιν λαμβάνομεν, καὶ τοὺς τῶν θείων καὶ μακαρίων ἀγώνων νόμους μανθάνομεν, καθ᾽ οὓς νομίμως ἀθλοῦντες τῶν ἀξιονίκων τῆς Χριστοῦ βασιλείας ἀξιούμεθα στεφάνων.

---

[78]ἀληθινὸν καὶ μόνον CCSG
[79]τῆς CCSG
[80]ἐπ᾽ ἂν CCSG

acknowledgement of God and the transformation of the faithful from evil and an absence of discernment to virtue and knowledge. For the entrance into the Church indicates not only the conversion [625] of the faithless to "the true" and "only God"[132] but also the correction through repentance of each of us who believe but still disobey the commandments of the Lord through our undisciplined conduct and shameful lives. For any man, whether a murderer or an adulterer or a [630] thief, whether "haughty,"[133] "boastful," "insolent," greedy, avaricious, "slanderous," vengeful, inclined to anger and wrath, abusive, or an extortionist, whether defamatory, given to envy, or a drunkard—but, let me not prolong the discourse by enumerating all the forms of evil—simply any man who had been held by any sort of evil but [CCSG 39; voluntarily ceases to be held by its pursuit and to act according to [635] its purpose and who changes his life for the better, choosing virtue rather than evil—let such a man be properly and truly perceived and said to enter with Christ, our God and high-priest, into virtue, which is figuratively perceived to be the Church. [640]

(10) What is the Symbolism of the Divine Readings

And the teacher said that the divine readings of the all-sacred books points towards the divine and blessed purposes and decrees of the all-holy God, through which each one of us receives "guidelines for living"[134] in proportion to the power within us.[135] We also learn [645] the rules of the divine and blessed contests, and when we "compete according to the rules,"[136] we are considered worthy of the victory-crowns of Christ's kingdom.

[132]Jn 17.3.
[133]Rom 1.30.
[134]Pseudo-Dionysius, *Ecclesiastical Hierarchy* 3.4. Maximus states that we interpret the law according to the power proportionate to us; he is conscious that not everyone in the Church will be able to interpret the laws in the same way. Some of the people in the congregation will obey some of the laws literally; others will interpret these same laws spiritually.
[135]Cf. Rom 12.6.
[136]2 Tim 2.5.

Κεφαλ. IA. Τίνος ἐστὶ σύμβολα τὰ θεῖα ᾄσματα

Τὴν δὲ πνευματικὴν τῶν θείων ἀσμάτων τερπνότητα, τὴν ἐμφαντικὴν δηλοῦν ἔφασκε τῶν θείων ἡδονὴν ἀγαθῶν, τὴν τὰς ψυχὰς πρὸς μὲν τὸν ἀκήρατον τοῦ Θεοῦ καὶ μακάριον ἀνακινοῦσαν ἔρωτα, πρὸς δὲ τὸ μῖσος τῆς ἁμαρτίας πλέον ἐγείρουσαν.

<689d> Κεφαλ. IB. Τί σημαίνουσιν αἱ τῆς εἰρήνης προσφωνήσεις

Διὰ δὲ τῶν γινομένων ἔνδοθεν ἐκ τοῦ ἱερατείου κελεύσει τοῦ ἀρχιερέως ἐφ᾽ ἑκάστῳ ἀναγνώσματι τῆς εἰρήνης ὑποφωνήσεων τὰς διὰ τῶν ἁγίων ἀγγέλων διακομιζομένας θείας ἀποδοχὰς δηλοῦσθαι ὁ σοφὸς διωρίζετο, δι᾽ ὧν ὁ Θεὸς ὁρίζει τῶν νομίμως ὑπὲρ τῆς ἀληθείας πρὸς τὰς ἀντικειμένας δυνάμεις ἀθλούντων τοὺς ἀγῶνας, τὰς ἀοράτους συμπλοκὰς <692a> διαλύων καὶ εἰρήνην διδοὺς ἐν τῇ καταργήσει τοῦ σώματος τῆς ἁμαρτίας καὶ τῶν ὑπὲρ ἀρετῆς πόνων τῆς ἀπαθείας τὴν χάριν τοῖς ἁγίοις ἀντιδιδούς, ἵνα τοῦ πολεμεῖν ἀφέμενοι, πρὸς γεωργίαν πνευματικήν, εἴτουν ἀρετῶν ἐργασίαν, τὰς τῆς ψυχῆς μετασκευάσωσι δυνάμεις, δι᾽ ὧν τὰ στίφη τῶν πονηρῶν πνευμάτων διέλυσαν, στρατηγοῦντος αὐτοῖς τοῦ Θεοῦ καὶ Λόγου, καὶ τὰ πικρὰ τοῦ διαβόλου καὶ δύσφυκτα[81] μηχανήματα διασκεδάζοντος.

Κεφαλ. ΙΓ. Τίνος ἰδικῶς ἐπὶ τοῦ καθ᾽ ἕκαστον σύμβολόν <692b> ἐστιν ἡ ἀνάγνωσις τοῦ ἁγίου Εὐαγγελίου καὶ τὰ μετ᾽ αὐτὴν μυστικά

Ὅθεν εὐθὺς μετὰ ταύτας, τὴν θείαν τοῦ ἁγίου Εὐαγγελίου ἀνάγνωσιν ἡ τῆς ἁγίας Ἐκκλησίας ἱερὰ διάταξις ἐνομοθέτησε γίγνεσθαι· ἰδικῶς μὲν τὴν ὑπὲρ τοῦ Λόγου τοῖς σπουδαίοις κακοπάθειαν εἰσηγουμένην, μεθ᾽ ἣν ὁ τῆς γνωστικῆς θεωρίας

---

[81] δυσάλυκτα CCSG

(11) What is the Symbolism of the Divine Songs

And he said that the spiritual delight of the divine songs indicates the vivid pleasure of the divine good things, which both awakens the [650] soul toward the pure and blessed love for God and stirs up a great hatred of sin.

(12) What the Pronouncements of Peace Signify

And the wise man explains that the salutations[137] of peace that come from within the sanctuary at the direction of the high-priest at each [655] reading indicate the divine acceptance conveyed by the holy angels. God ordains through these angels the contests of those who "compete according to the rules"[138] against the opposing powers, ending the invisible struggles and granting peace by the "bringing to nothing of the body."[139] In return for their toils for virtue and freedom [CCSG 41; from the passions, he gives grace to the saints in order that, now [660] that they have abandoned warfare, they might transfer the powers of the soul to spiritual fruitfulness, which is the life of virtue. The saints dispel the hordes of evil spirits through these powers, with God the Word as their general, who brings to nothing the piercing and treacherous machinations of the devil. [665]

(13) What is the Specific Symbolism, in Each Instance, of the Reading of the Holy Gospel and the Mystical Rites that Follow

Therefore, the sacred regulation of the holy Church legislates that the divine reading of the holy Gospel take place immediately after these things. Specifically, on the one hand, the reading introduces suffering for the sake of the word to the fervent. After the reading, [670] the Word of spiritual contemplation—as the high priest—comes

---

[137]ὑποφώνησις; in the chapter title the Greek term is προσφώνησις ("pronouncements"). Maximus here refers to the pronouncement of peace ("peace be unto all") and the response ("and with your spirit").

[138]2 Tim 2.5.

[139]Cf. Rom 6.6.

ὥσπερ ἀρχιερεὺς οὐρανόθεν ἐπιδημῶν αὐτοῖς Λόγος τῆς σαρκὸς αὐτοῖς ὥσπερ τινὰ κόσμον αἰσθητὸν συστέλλει τὸ φρόνημα. τοὺς ἔτι πρὸς γῆν κατανεύοντας λογισμοὺς[82] ἀπωθούμενος καὶ πρὸς τὴν τῶν νοητῶν ἐποψίαν ἐντεῦθεν διὰ τῆς τῶν θυρῶν κλείσεως καὶ τῆς εἰσόδου τῶν ἁγίων μυστηρίων αὐτοὺς ἀγαγών, λόγων τε καὶ πραγμάτων μύσαντας ἤδη τὰς αἰσθήσεις καὶ ἔξω σαρκὸς καὶ κόσμου γεγενημένους, τὰ <692c> ἀπόρρητα διδάσκει· συναχθέντας ἤδη[83] διὰ τοῦ ἀσπασμοῦ πρὸς ἑαυτούς τε καὶ αὐτὸν καὶ μόνην ἀντεισάγοντας αὐτῷ τῆς περὶ αὐτοὺς πολλῆς εὐεργεσίας εὐγνωμόνως τὴν ὑπὲρ τῆς ἑαυτῶν σωτηρίας εὐχαριστήριον ὁμολογίαν, ἣν τὸ θεῖον τῆς πίστεως αἰνίττεται Σύμβολον. εἶτα τοῖς ἀγγέλοις ἐναριθμίους αὐτοὺς καταστήσας διὰ τοῦ Τρισαγίου καὶ τὴν αὐτὴν ἐκείνοις ἐπιστήμην τῆς ἁγιαστικῆς θεολογίας αὐτοῖς χαρισάμενος τῷ Θεῷ καὶ Πατρὶ προσάγει, υἱοθετηθέντας τῷ Πνεύματι διὰ τῆς προσευχῆς, δι᾽ ἧς Πατέρα καλεῖν τὸν Θεὸν ἠξιώθησαν. κἀντεῦθεν πάλιν ὥσπερ ἐπιστημόνως ἤδη τοὺς ἐν τοῖς οὖσι πάντας λόγους περάσαντας, πρὸς τὴν ἄγνωστον ἀγνώστως διὰ τοῦ Εἷς ἅγιος καὶ τῶν ἑξῆς ἄγει μονάδα, τῇ χάριτι ἑνωθέντας καὶ κατὰ μέθεξιν πρὸς αὐτὴν ὁμοιωθέντας <692d> τῇ κατὰ δύναμιν ἀδιαιρέτῳ ταυτότητι.

---

[82]λογισμοὺς, ὡς κατηχουμένους, αυτῶν CCSG
[83]ἤδη πρότερον CCSG

from heaven to dwell among the people[140] and brings to an end "the mind set on flesh"[141]—as the sensible realm—because, while the people are being instructed, [the Word] drives away from them the arguments that still bow[142] towards the earth. And from there [the Word] leads them to the vision of the intelligible things through the closing of the doors and the entrance of the holy mysteries. [The Word] teaches unspeakable things to "those who have" now "shut out the sense perception" of speech and action "and have gone outside the flesh and the world."[143] They are first reconciled through the kiss of peace with one another and also with him, and in gratitude they next proceed to the confession of thanks for their salvation in return for his great kindness toward them, which the divine symbol of faith[144] communicates mysteriously. Then [the Word] counts them among the angels through the Trisagion[145] and grants to them the same knowledge in ascribing holiness to God.[146] [The Word] brings them to God the Father[147] because they have been adopted in the Spirit through the prayer through which they are deemed worthy to call God "Father." And from there, when by knowledge they have passed through all the principles in the things that exist, next [the Word] leads them to the unknowable Monad in an unknowable way through the singing of the "One Is Holy." And they are deified by grace and made like the undivided identity by participation with the Monad to the best of their ability.

[CCSG 42]
[675]
[680]
[685]
[690]

[140]The moment that the priest comes to read the Gospel book represents the coming of God the Word.

[141]Rom 8.6.

[142]Cf. 2 Cor 10.5.

[143]Gregory Nazianzus, *Oration* 2.7.

[144]I.e., the Nicene-Constantinopolitan Creed.

[145]τρισάγιος; the *Tersanctus* or the hymn proclaiming "Holy, Holy, Holy" is the Lord (cf. Is 6.3 and Rev 4.8).

[146]ἁγιαστικῆς θεολογίας; this could be translated literally as "sanctifying theology," i.e., a knowledge in ascribing holiness to God.

[147]Lit. "the God and Father."

Κεφαλ. ΙΔ. Τίνος ἐστὶ σύμβολον, κατὰ τὸ γενικῶς σημαινόμενον, ἡ θεία τοῦ ἁγίου Εὐαγγελίου ἀνάγνωσις

Γενικῶς δὲ τὴν τοῦ κόσμου τούτου συντέλειαν ὑποσημαίνουσαν. μετὰ γὰρ τὴν θείαν τοῦ ἁγίου Εὐαγγελίου ἀνάγνωσιν ὅ τε ἀρχιερεὺς κάτεισι τοῦ θρόνου, καὶ ἡ τῶν κατηχουμένων καὶ ἡ τῶν λοιπῶν <693a> τῶν ἀναξίων τῆς θείας τῶν δειχθησομένων μυστηρίων θεωρίας ἀπόλυσίς τε καὶ ἐκβολὴ διὰ τῶν λειτουργῶν γίγνεται, σημαίνουσα καὶ προτυποῦσα δι᾽ ἑαυτῆς τὴν ἀλήθειαν, ἧς εἰκὼν ὑπάρχει καὶ τύπος, καὶ οἷον ἐν τούτοις βοῶσα, ὅτι μετὰ τὸ κηρυχθῆναι τὸ Εὐαγγέλιον, καθὼς γέγραπται, τῆς βασιλείας ἐν ὅλῃ τῇ οἰκουμένῃ εἰς μαρτύριον πᾶσι τοῖς ἔθνεσι, τότε ἥξει τὸ τέλος, παραγινομένου κατὰ τὴν δευτέραν αὐτοῦ παρουσίαν, ἐξ οὐρανῶν δηλαδή, μετὰ δόξης πολλῆς τοῦ μεγάλου Θεοῦ καὶ Σωτῆρος ἡμῶν Ἰησοῦ Χριστοῦ· αὐτὸς γὰρ ὁ Κύριος ἐν φωνῇ ἀρχαγγέλου καὶ ἐν σάλπιγγι Θεοῦ καταβήσεται ἀπ᾽ οὐρανοῦ, φησὶν ὁ θεῖος Ἀπόστολος· καὶ ποιοῦντος ἐκδίκησιν ἐν τοῖς ὑπεναντίοις καὶ ἀφορίζοντος διὰ τῶν ἁγίων ἀγγέλων τοὺς πιστοὺς ἀπὸ τῶν ἀπίστων, <693b> καὶ ἀπὸ τῶν δικαίων τοὺς ἀδίκους, καὶ τῶν ἁγίων τοὺς ἐναγεῖς, καὶ ἁπλῶς, ἵνα συνελὼν εἴπω, τῶν Πνεύματι Θεοῦ στοιχησάντων, τοὺς ὀπίσω σαρκὸς πορευθέντας, καὶ ἐπ᾽ αἰῶσι ἀπείροις τε καὶ ἀτελευτήτοις, ὡς ἡ τῶν θείων λογίων ἀλήθειά φησι, κατ᾽ ἀξίαν τῶν βεβιωμένων ἑκάστῳ δικαίαν ἀποδιδόντος[84] τὴν ἀμοιβήν.

---

[84]ἀποδιδούντος CCSG

(14) What is the General Symbolism of the Divine Reading of the Holy Gospel [CCSG 43]

Generally, on the other hand, the reading foreshadows the end of this world. For after the divine reading of the holy Gospel, the high priest comes down from the throne, and the ministers release and [695] dismiss the catechumens and the rest of those who are unworthy of the divine contemplation of the mysteries that are about to be presented. The dismissal signifies and prefigures in itself the truth—for the dismissal is an image and representation and proclaims the image in this part of the liturgy—that, even as it is written, "after [700] the gospel of the kingdom has been preached in the whole world as a testimony to all the nations, then the end will come."[148] He will appear "with all glory"[149] at his second coming from the heavens, that is "our great God and Savior Jesus Christ."[150] "For the Lord himself will descend from heaven, with the archangel's call, and with [705] the sound of the trumpet of God,"[151] as the divine apostle says. And he will "exact vengeance"[152] on his adversaries, and he will separate [CCSG 44] by the holy angels the faithful from the faithless, "the unjust" from the just, and "the accursed from the saints,"[153] and—if I may speak simply and concisely—"those who walk after the flesh"[154] from [710] "those who keep in step with the Spirit of God,"[155] even for indefinite and unending ages. He will then render a just recompense to each of those who have lived according to their worth, as the truth of the divine oracles affirms.[156]

[148]Mt 24.14.
[149]Mt 24.30.
[150]Tit 2.13.
[151]1 Thess 4.16.
[152]Lk 18.7.
[153]Pseudo-Dionysius, *Epistle* 10.
[154]2 Pet 2.10.
[155]Gal 5.25.
[156]Cf. Rom 3.2.

Κεφαλ. ΙΕ. Τίνος σύμβολόν ἐστι ἡ κλεῖσις τῶν θυρῶν τῆς ἁγίας Ἐκκλησίας, ἡ μετὰ τὸ ἅγιον Εὐαγγέλιον γιγνομένη

Ἡ δὲ μετὰ τὴν ἱερὰν ἀνάγνωσιν τοῦ ἁγίου Εὐαγγελίου καὶ τὴν ἐκβολὴν τῶν κατηχουμένων γινομένη <693c> κλεῖσις τῶν θυρῶν τῆς ἁγίας τοῦ Θεοῦ Ἐκκλησίας, τήν τε τῶν ὑλικῶν δηλοῖ πάροδον, καὶ τὴν γενησομένην μετὰ τὸν φοβερὸν ἐκεῖνον, ἀφορισμόν, καὶ τὴν φοβερωτέραν ψῆφον εἰς τὸν νοητὸν κόσμον, ἤτοι τὸν νυμφῶνα τοῦ Χριστοῦ, τῶν ἀξίων εἴσοδον, καὶ τὴν ἐν ταῖς αἰσθήσεσι τῆς κατὰ τὴν ἀπάτην ἐνεργείας τελείαν ἀποβολήν.

Κεφαλ. ΙΣ. Τί σημαίνει ἡ τῶν ἁγίων Μυστηρίων εἴσοδος

Ἡ δὲ τῶν ἁγίων καὶ σεπτῶν Μυστηρίων εἴσοδος ἀρχὴ καὶ προοίμιόν ἐστιν (ὡς ὁ μέγας ἐκεῖνος ἔφασκε γέρων) τῆς γενησομένης ἐν οὐρανοῖς καινῆς διδασκαλίας περὶ τῆς οἰκονομίας τοῦ Θεοῦ τῆς εἰς ἡμᾶς, καὶ ἀποκάλυψις τοῦ ἐν ἀδύτοις τῆς θείας <693d> κρυφιότητος ὄντος μυστηρίου τῆς ἡμῶν σωτηρίας. οὐ γὰρ μὴ πίω, φησὶ πρὸς τοὺς ἑαυτοῦ μαθητὰς ὁ Θεὸς καὶ Λόγος, ἀπ᾽ ἄρτι ἐκ τοῦ γεννήματος τῆς ἀμπέλου, ἕως τῆς ἡμέρας ἐκείνης, ὅταν αὐτὸ πίνω μεθ᾽ ὑμῶν καινὸν ἐν τῇ βασιλείᾳ τοῦ Πατρὸς ἐμοῦ.

Κεφαλ. ΙΖ. Τίνος ἐστὶ σύμβολον ὁ θεῖος ἀσπασμός

Ὁ δὲ πᾶσι προσφωνούμενος πνευματικὸς ἀσπασμὸς τὴν ἐσομένην πάντων πρὸς ἀλλήλους ἐν τῷ καιρῷ <696a> τῆς τῶν μελλόντων ἀρρήτων ἀγαθῶν ἀποκαλύψεως, κατὰ πίστιν τε καὶ ἀγάπην, ὁμόνοιάν τε καὶ ὁμογνωμοσύνην καὶ ταυτότητα λογικήν, δι᾽ ἣν τὴν πρὸς τὸν Λόγον καὶ Θεὸν οἰκείωσιν οἱ ἄξιοι δέχονται, προτυποῖ καὶ προδιαγράφει. Λόγου γὰρ σύμβολον τὸ στόμα, καθ᾽

(15) What is the Symbolism of the Closing of the Doors of the Holy Church after the Reading of the Holy Gospel

The closing of the doors of the holy Church of God, which takes place after the sacred reading of the holy Gospel and the dismissal of [715] the catechumens, indicates the passing from material things and the entrance of those who are worthy into the intelligible realm—that [CCSG 45] is, into the bridal chamber of Christ. This shall take place after that frightful separation and the even more frightful sentence. The clos- [720] ing of the doors also indicates the final rejection[157] of the deceitful activity of sense perception.

(16) What the Entrance of the Holy Mysteries Signifies

The entrance of the holy and revered mysteries is, as the great elder said, the beginning and prelude of the new teaching that will be in heaven, of God's dispensation toward us. It is also the revelation of the mystery of our salvation, which is in the "inner sanctuaries"[158] [725] of the divine hiddenness. For God the Word says to his disciples, "I shall not drink again of the fruit of the vine until that day when I drink it new with you in my Father's kingdom."[159]

(17) What is the Symbolism of the Kiss of Peace   [CCSG 46]

The spiritual kiss of peace, which is addressed to all the people, prefigures and portrays in advance the unanimity, agreement, and [730] identity in rationality that we all shall possess toward one another at the time when the unspeakable blessings to come will be revealed according to faith and love; and it is through this identity that the worthy receive kinship with God the Word. For the mouth is a symbol of reason—the reason by which in fact all who participate [735]

---

[157]ἀποβολή; "discarding." This term is closely related to ἐκβολή, which was translated "dismissal" at the beginning of the chapter.

[158]Pseudo-Dionysius, *On the Divine Names* 4.22.

[159]Mt 26.29.

ὃν μάλιστα πᾶσιν ἅπαντες οἱ λόγου μετειληφότες, ὡς λογικοί, καὶ τῷ πρώτῳ καὶ μόνῳ Λόγῳ καὶ παντὸς αἰτίῳ λόγου συμφύονται.

Κεφαλ. ΙΗ. Τί σημαίνει τὸ θεῖον τῆς πίστεως Σύμβολον

Ἡ δὲ τοῦ θείου Συμβόλου τῆς πίστεως γινομένη παρὰ πάντων ὁμολογία τὴν ἐφ᾽ οἷς ἐσώθημεν παραδόξοις <696b> λόγοις τε καὶ τρόποις τῆς πανσόφου περὶ ἡμᾶς τοῦ Θεοῦ προνοίας γενησομένην μυστικὴν εὐχαριστίαν κατὰ τὸν αἰῶνα τὸν μέλλοντα προσημαίνει, δι᾽ ἧς εὐγνώμονας ἐπὶ τῇ θείᾳ εὐεργεσίᾳ ἑαυτοὺς συνιστῶσιν οἱ ἄξιοι, πλὴν ταύτης τῶν περὶ αὐτοὺς ἀπείρων θείων ἀγαθῶν ἀντεισαγαγεῖν ἄλλο τι[85] καθ᾽ ὁτιοῦν οὐκ ἔχοντες.

Κεφαλ. ΙΘ. Τί σημαίνει ἡ τοῦ Τρισαγίου δοξολογία

Ἡ δὲ γινομένη τρισσὴ τοῦ ἁγιασμοῦ τῆς θείας ὑμνολογίας ἐκβόησις παρὰ παντὸς τοῦ πιστοῦ λαοῦ τὴν πρὸς τὰς ἀσωμάτους καὶ νοερὰς δυνάμεις κατὰ τὸ μέλλον φανησομένην ἕνωσίν τε καὶ ἰσοτιμίαν παραδηλοῖ, <696c> καθ᾽ ἣν συμφώνως ταῖς ἄνω δυνάμεσι διὰ ταυτότητα τῆς ἀτρέπτου περὶ Θεὸν ἀεικινησίας τρισὶν ἁγιασμοῖς ὑμνεῖν τε καὶ ἁγιάζειν τὴν τρισυπόστατον μίαν θεότητα διδαχθήσεται τῶν ἀνθρώπων ἡ φύσις.

Κεφαλ. Κ. Τίνος ἐστὶ σύμβολον ἡ ἁγία προσευχὴ τοῦ Πάτερ ἡμῶν ὁ ἐν τοῖς οὐρανοῖς...[86]

Ἡ δὲ παναγία τε καὶ σεπτὴ τοῦ μεγάλου καὶ μακαρίου Θεοῦ καὶ Πατρὸς ἐπίκλησις τῆς δοθησομένης ἐνυποστάτου τε καὶ ἐνυπάρκτου κατὰ δωρεὰν καὶ χάριν τοῦ ἁγίου Πνεύματος υἱοθεσίας ἐστὶ σύμβολον, καθ᾽ ἣν πάσης ὑπερνικωμένης τε καὶ καλυπτομένης <696d> ἀνθρωπίνης ἰδιότητος τῇ ἐπιφοιτήσει τῆς χάριτος υἱοὶ Θεοῦ χρηματίσουσί τε καὶ ἔσονται πάντες οἱ ἅγιοι,

---

[85]om. CCSG
[86]ὁ ἐν τοῖς οὐρανοῖς om. CCSG

in rationality are united to all things as rational beings and united to the first and only Word and the Cause of all rationality.

(18) What the Divine Symbol of Faith Signifies

The confession of the divine symbol of faith that is confessed by all foretells—in the miraculous words and ways[160] of the all-wise provi- [740] dence of God toward us by which we have been saved—the mystical Eucharist that shall be in the age to come. And it will be through this Eucharist that the worthy will show themselves to be grateful for the divine kindness, inasmuch as aside from this they have no way to return thanks for the infinite divine blessings they have received.

(19) What the Doxology of the Trisagion Signifies   [CCSG 47]

The threefold proclamation of holiness, exclaimed by all the faith- [745] ful people in the divine hymn, intimates the oneness and equality of honor that shall be revealed to the incorporeal and intellectual powers[161] in the future. Then human nature will be taught to sing in harmony with the powers above and to ascribe holiness to the one deity in three hypostases, and this singing will be in harmony [750] because of the identity of the three consecrations with the unchangeable, ceaseless motion around God.

[20] What is the Symbolism of the Holy Prayer, the "Our Father"

The all-holy and revered invocation of our great and blessed God the Father is a symbol of the subsistent and immanent adoption, which will be given according to the gift and grace of the Holy Spirit. When [755] this adoption occurs, every human particularity will be overcome and concealed, and all the saints will be called and will be sons of God by the grace that has come upon them, as many as washed

---

[160]λόγοις τὲ καὶ τρόποις; elsewhere these terms are translated "principles" and "modes."

[161]Cf. Eph 3.10.

ὅσοι δι᾽ ἀρετῶν ἀπ᾽ ἐντεῦθεν ἤδη τῷ θείῳ τῆς ἀγαθότητος κάλλει
ἑαυτοὺς λαμπρῶς τε καὶ ἐπιδόξως ἐφαίδρυναν.

Κεφαλ. ΚΑ. Τί σημαίνει τὸ τέλος τῆς μυστικῆς ἱερουργίας τῶν
ἐκφωνουμένων ὕμνων, τουτέστιν Εἷς ἅγιος, εἷς Κύριος,[87] καὶ τὰ
ἑξῆς

Ἡ δὲ κατὰ τὸ τέλος τῆς μυστικῆς ἱερουργίας παρὰ παντὸς τοῦ λαοῦ
γινομένη τοῦ Εἷς ἅγιος καὶ τῶν ἑξῆς ὁμολογία τὴν ὑπὲρ λόγον καὶ
νοῦν πρὸς τὸ ἓν τῆς θείας ἁπλότητος κρύφιον γενησομένην τῶν
μυστικῶς τε καὶ σοφῶς κατὰ Θεὸν τετελεσμένων συναγωγήν τε
καὶ ἕνωσιν δηλοῖ, ἐν τῷ <697a> ἀφθάρτῳ τῶν νοητῶν αἰῶνι καθ᾽
ὃν τῆς ἀφανοῦς καὶ ὑπεραρρήτου δόξης τὸ φῶς ἐνοπτεύοντες τῆς
μακαρίας μετὰ τῶν ἄνω δυνάμεων, καὶ αὐτοὶ δεκτικοὶ γίγνονται
καθαρότητος.

Μεθ᾽ ἥν, ὡς τέλος πάντων, ἡ τοῦ μυστηρίου μετάδοσις γίνεται
μεταποιοῦσα πρὸς ἑαυτὴν καὶ ὁμοίους τῷ κατ᾽ αἰτίαν ἀγαθῷ κατὰ
χάριν καὶ μέθεξιν ἀποφαίνουσα τοὺς ἀξίως μεταλαμβάνοντας,
ἐν μηδενὶ αὐτοῦ λειπομένους, κατὰ τὸ ἐφικτὸν ἀνθρώποις καὶ
ἐνδεχόμενον. ὥστε καὶ αὐτοὺς δύνασθαι εἶναί τε καὶ καλεῖσθαι
θέσει κατὰ τὴν χάριν θεούς, διὰ τὸν αὐτοὺς ὅλως[88] πληρώσαντα
ὅλον Θεὸν καὶ μηδὲν αὐτῶν τῆς αὐτοῦ παρουσίας κενὸν
καταλείψαντα.

---

[87]εἷς Κύριος om. CCSG
[88]ὅλως ἑαυτοῦ CCSG

themselves brightly and gloriously from then on[162] in the divine beauty of goodness through the virtues.

[21] What the Singing of Hymns at the Conclusion of the [CCSG 48] Mystical Liturgy Signifies—that is, the "One is Holy" and the Hymns that Follow

The confession of the "One is Holy" by all the people and the hymns [760] that follow at the conclusion of the mystical liturgy indicate the assembling and oneness of those who have been mystically and wisely perfected by God in the immortal age of the intelligible realm—the assembling and oneness, which will be beyond reason and the mind, with the One hidden in divine simplicity. In this age, [765] by contemplating the light of the invisible and more than ineffable glory, even they will become recipients of the blessed cleansing with the powers above.

After the cleansing comes the imparting of the mystery[163] at the conclusion of all these things. The mystery transforms those who [770] partake in a worthy manner into itself and, by grace and participation, renders them similar to the one who is good as the cause of everything that is good.[164] And they are "lacking in nothing"[165] from him in as far as it is possible and attainable for men, so that even they are able to be and to be called gods by adoption according to grace, because the whole of God fills the whole of them with himself and [CCSG 49] leaves nothing in them empty from his presence. [775]

---

[162]I.e., from the moment of baptism.

[163]Maximus here refers to the distribution of the sacrament. Cf. Pseudo-Dionysius, *Ecclesiastical Hierarchy* 3.1.

[164]τῷ κατ᾽ αἰτίαν ἀγαθῷ; this could be translated literally: "to the one who is good according to cause."

[165]Jas 1.4.

<697b> Κεφαλ. ΚΒ. Πῶς[89] καὶ τίνι τρόπῳ καὶ ἡ τῆς ψυχῆς καθ᾽ ἑαυτὴν νοουμένης ἐπὶ τοῦ καθ᾽ ἕκαστον ἰδικῶς ἐκθεωτικὴ καὶ τελειοποιὸς διὰ τῶν εἰρημένων θεωρεῖται κατάστασις

Δεῦρο δὴ οὖν διὰ τῶν αὐτῶν ὁδῷ καὶ τάξει βαίνοντες πάλιν τὰ αὐτὰ καὶ περὶ ψυχῆς γνωστικῆς θεωρήσωμεν, καὶ συναναβῆναι μικρὸν κατὰ δύναμιν τῷ λόγῳ μετ᾽ εὐλαβείας πρὸς ὑψηλοτέραν θεωρίαν, σκοπῆσαί τε καὶ κατανοῆσαι πῶς οἱ θεῖοι τῆς ἁγίας Ἐκκλησίας θεσμοὶ τὴν ψυχὴν ἐπὶ τὴν ἑαυτῆς τελειότητα δι᾽ ἀληθοῦς καὶ ἐνεργοῦς γνώσεως ἄγουσι, ποθοῦντα τὸν νοῦν καὶ βουλόμενον, Θεοῦ χειραγωγοῦντος (εἰ δοκεῖ) μὴ κωλύσωμεν.

<697c> Κεφαλ. ΚΓ. Ὅτι[90] σύμβολον τῶν κατὰ ψυχὴν ἀρετῶν ἐστιν ἡ πρώτη εἴσοδος τῆς ἁγίας συνάξεως

Ἄθρει τοιγαροῦν, ὅστις τῆς μακαρίας τοῦ Χριστοῦ σοφίας γνήσιος καθέστηκας ἐραστής, νοὸς ὀφθαλμοῖς κατὰ τὴν πρώτην εἴσοδον τῆς ἁγίας συνάξεως ἀπὸ τῆς ἔξωθεν τῶν ὑλικῶν πλάνης καὶ ταραχῆς, κατὰ τὸ γεγραμμένον Γυναῖκες ἐρχόμεναι ἀπὸ θέας, δεῦτε, τῆς ἐν εἴδει καὶ σχήματι, φημὶ κατὰ τὴν πρόσοψιν τῶν αἰσθητῶν περιπλανήσεως· οὐ γὰρ θεωρίαν εἰπεῖν ἀληθές, κατὰ τοὺς ἀσόφους τῶν παρ᾽ Ἕλλησι λεγομένων σοφῶν (μηδὲ γὰρ σοφοὶ κληθεῖεν ποτε πρὸς ἡμῶν οἱ τὸν Θεὸν γνῶναι διὰ τῶν αὐτοῦ ποιημάτων μὴ δυνηθέντες ἢ μὴ βουληθέντες) τῶν αἰσθητῶν λέγω[91] τὴν ἐπιφάνειαν, <697d> καθ᾽ ἣν ὁ διηνεκὴς τῶν αἰσθητῶν πρὸς ἄλληλα συνέστηκε πόλεμος, πᾶσι τὴν δι᾽ ἀλλήλων φθορὰν ἐνεργῶν, πάντων φθειρόντων ἄλληλα καὶ ἐν ἀλλήλοις φθειρομένων· καὶ τοῦτο μόνον πάγιον ἔχοντα,[92] τὸ ἀστατεῖν καὶ

---

[89] πῶς τε CCSG
[90] τίνος CCSG
[91] τῶν αἰσθητῶν λέγω om. CCSG
[92] ἐχόντων CCSG

[22] How and in What Manner the Deifying and Perfecting Restoration of the Soul (When the Soul is Considered by Itself and in What concerns Each Properly and Individually) is Contemplated in the Above

Come then, proceeding through the previous subjects in a systematic and orderly fashion, let us contemplate again the same things in relation to the spiritual soul. And, with God leading by the hand, as it were, let us ascend in this discourse by a little and to the best of our ability and with reverence toward a higher contemplation, not forbidding the mind, which longs to peer into and desires to learn [780] how the divine precepts of the holy Church lead the soul to its own perfection through true and effective knowledge.

[23] What is the Symbolism of the First Entrance of the Holy Synaxis in Reference to the Virtues of the Soul

Therefore, you who have become a genuine lover of the blessed wis- [785] dom of Christ, look with the eyes of the mind upon the first entrance [CCSG 50] of the holy synaxis, which is the first entrance "from outside" the wandering and "disturbance"[166] of material things—as it is written, "you women who come away from sight, come here!"[167] I am speaking about coming away from the wandering of the sensible things in the appearance of their form and shape. (For, to state the truth, I am not speaking about the contemplation of the unwise who are [790] said to be wise among the Greeks; for, they should not be called wise among us who are neither able nor willing to know God through "the things that have been made"[168] by him.) Because of this wandering, a perpetual "war" of the sensible things "with one another"[169] has arisen, working destruction in everything through one another. The sensible things all destroy one another and are destroyed by one [795] another, and they possess firmly only this: to be unsettled and to be

[166]Gregory of Nazianzus, *Oration* 27.3.
[167]Is 27.11.
[168]Cf. Rom 1.20.
[169]Gregory of Nazianzus, *Oration* 27.6.

φθείρεσθαι καὶ μηδέποτε συμβαίνειν ἀλλήλοις κατὰ διαμονὴν ἄμαχον δύνασθαι καὶ ἀστασίαστον, ἐρχομένην τε τὴν ψυχὴν καὶ προτροπάδην φεύγουσαν καὶ ὥσπερ εἰς Ἐκκλησίαν καὶ ἄσυλον εἰρήνης ἀνάκτορον τὴν ἐν πνεύματι φυσικὴν θεωρίαν τὴν ἄμαχον καὶ πάσης ἐλευθέραν ταραχῆς μετὰ[93] Λόγου τε καὶ ὑπὸ τοῦ Λόγου τοῦ μεγάλου καὶ <700a> ἀληθοῦς ἡμῶν Θεοῦ καὶ ἀρχιερέως εἰσερχομένην.

Καὶ ὡς διὰ συμβόλων τῶν γινομένων θείων ἀναγνωσμάτων, τοὺς[94] τῶν ὄντων διδασκομένην λόγους καὶ τὸ θαυμαστὸν καὶ μέγα τῆς ἐν νόμῳ καὶ προφήταις δηλουμένης θείας προνοίας μυστήριον, καθ᾽ ἕκαστόν τε δεξαμένην ὑπὲρ τῆς ἐν τούτοις καλῆς μαθητείας θεόθεν διὰ τῶν ἁγίων δυνάμεων νοερῶς κατὰ διάνοιαν αὐτῇ διαλεγομένων τὰς εἰρηνοδώρους σημειώσεις μετὰ τῆς ῥωστικῆς καὶ συντηρητικῆς θέλξεως τῆς θείας καὶ διαπύρου κατὰ Θεὸν ἐφέσεως, διὰ τῆς μυστικῶς ὑπαδομένης αὐτῇ νοητῶς τῶν θείων ἀσμάτων ἡδονῆς.

Πάλιν ἐκ τούτων μεταβαίνουσαν <700b> καὶ συναγομένην ἐπὶ τὴν μίαν καὶ μόνην καὶ ἑνιαίως τούτους συλλαμβάνουσαν τοὺς λόγους κορυφήν, λέγω δὲ[95] τὸ ἅγιον Εὐαγγέλιον, ἐν ᾧ πάντες τῆς τε προνοίας καὶ τῶν ὄντων οἱ λόγοι κατὰ μίαν περιοχῆς δύναμιν ἑνοειδῶς προϋφεστήκασι.

Μεθ᾽ ὃ κατ᾽ αἴσθησιν θείαν αὐτὸν ὁρᾶν ἔνεστι πάλιν θεμιτὸν τοῖς φιλοθέοις ἀταρβήτοις νοὸς ὄμμασι παραγινόμενον οὐρανόθεν αὐτῇ τὸν Λόγον καὶ Θεόν, ὡς ἡ τοῦ ἀρχιερέως ἀπὸ τοῦ θρόνου τοῦ ἱερατικοῦ σημαίνει κατάβασις, καὶ τέλειον αὐτῆς διακρίνοντα

---

[93] μετὰ τοῦ CCSG
[94] τούς τε CCSG
[95] δὴ CCSG

destroyed and never to be able to come to an agreement permanently with one another without conflict and unsettledness. And the soul, coming and fleeing precipitously, enters into the natural contemplation that is without conflict and free from every disturbance, in the [800] Spirit and with the Word and by the Word of our great and true God and high priest, even as it enters into the Church, the sanctuary and temple of peace.

And through the symbols of the divine readings that are performed, the soul is taught the principles of the things that exist and the marvelous and great mystery of the divine providence revealed in the Law and the prophets. And, in each principle concerning the beautiful instruction given by God in these mysteries through the holy powers who converse intellectually with the soul according to understanding, the soul receives the peace-granting significations with the strengthening and protecting enchantment[170] of the divine [810] and ardent desire toward God. This occurs through the intelligible pleasure of the divine hymns that the soul mystically accompanies in song. [CCSG 51] [805]

Again, the soul continues on from these things and is brought to the one and only summit[171] that receives these principles into a unity—I am speaking about the holy Gospel, in which all principles [815] of providence and of the things that exist preexist in a unified form in the power that encompasses everything.

After this it is possible and permitted by God to see by divine discernment[172] and with the devout and fearless eyes of the mind God the Word himself. He comes from heaven to the soul (which the descent of the high-priest from the sacerdotal throne signifies) and separates the soul's perfected part (as catechumens) and the [820]

---

[170]Cf. Pseudo-Dionysius, *Celestial Hierarchy* 3.7, 4.3; Methodius of Olympus, *Symposium* 11.

[171]Cf. Pseudo-Dionysius, *On the Divine Names* 4.28.

[172]Cf. Phil 1.9, which is the only occurrence of this Greek term in the New Testament. [It can also mean simply "perception" (αἴσθησις), especially sensory perception, but it is also used by Plato and others to refer to a spiritual or noetic perception of immaterial realities.—*Ed.*].

κατηχουμένων δίκην τοὺς ἔτι τὴν αἴσθησιν καὶ τὸ κατ' αὐτὴν
μεριστὸν φαντασιουμένους λογισμούς.

Κἀντεῦθεν πάλιν ἔξω γενομένην τῶν αἰσθητῶν, ὡς ἡ τῶν
θυρῶν τῆς ἁγίας τοῦ Θεοῦ Ἐκκλησίας νοεῖν ὑποτίθεται κλεῖσις, ἐπὶ
<700c> τὴν δηλουμένην διὰ τῆς εἰσόδου τῶν ἀρρήτων μυστηρίων
ἄϋλον καὶ ἁπλῆν καὶ ἀναλλοίωτον καὶ θεοειδῆ καὶ παντὸς
ἐλευθέραν εἴδους καὶ σχήματος ἐπιστήμην τῶν νοητῶν ἄγοντα,
καθ' ἣν συναγαγοῦσαν πρὸς μὲν ἑαυτῆς⁹⁶ τὰς οἰκείας δυνάμεις,
πρὸς δὲ τὸν Λόγον ἑαυτὴν καταντᾷ,⁹⁷ διὰ τοῦ νοεροῦ ἀσπασμοῦ
ἑνώσασαν τοὺς περὶ ἑαυτὴν⁹⁸ ἀρρήτους τῆς σωτηρίας καὶ λόγους
καὶ τρόπους, διὰ τοῦ Συμβόλου τῆς πίστεως εὐχαρίστως ὁμολογεῖν
ἐκδιδάσκοντα.

Ἐπὶ τούτοις δὲ πάλιν, ὡς ἤδη λοιπὸν κατὰ δύναμιν ἁπλῆν
καὶ ἀδιαίρετον διὰ μαθητείας γνώσει περιλαβοῦσαν τούς τε τῶν
αἰσθητῶν καὶ τῶν νοητῶν λόγους, ἐπὶ τὴν γνῶσιν τῆς ἐκφανοῦς
αὐτὴν ἄγοντα θεολογίας μετὰ τὴν πάντων διάβασιν καὶ <700d> τὴν
ἴσην τοῖς ἀγγέλοις κατὰ τὸ ἐφικτὸν αὐτῇ παρεχόμενον νόησιν καὶ
τοσοῦτον διδάσκοντα σωφρόνως αὐτήν, ὅσον εἰδέναι Θεὸν ἕνα,
μίαν οὐσίαν, ὑποστάσεις τρεῖς· μονάδα οὐσίας τρισυπόστατον καὶ
τριάδα ὑποστάσεων ὁμοούσιον, μονάδα ἐν τριάδι καὶ τριάδα ἐν
μονάδι· οὐκ ἄλλην καὶ ἄλλην, οὐδ' ἄλλην παρ' ἄλλην, οὐδὲ δι'
ἄλλης ἄλλην, οὐδ' ἄλλην ἐν ἄλλῃ, οὐδὲ ἐξ ἄλλης ἄλλην· ἀλλὰ
τὴν αὐτὴν ἐν ἑαυτῇ, καὶ καθ' ἑαυτὴν ἐφ' ἑαυτῇ, ἑαυτῇ ταύτην⁹⁹
καὶ μονάδα καὶ τριάδα ἀσύγχυτον¹⁰⁰ τε καὶ ἀσυγχύτως¹⁰¹ τὴν
ἕνωσιν ἔχουσαν καὶ τὴν διάκρισιν ἀδιαίρετόν τε καὶ ἀμέριστον·

⁹⁶ἑαυτὴν CCSG
⁹⁷κατὰ νοῦν CCSG
⁹⁸αὐτὴν CCSG
⁹⁹ταυτὸν CCSG
¹⁰⁰ἀσυνθετόν CCSG
¹⁰¹ἀσυγχύτον CCSG

thoughts that are still formed by sense perception and are divisible according to sense perception.

And then, again coming away from outside the sensible things (which the closing of the doors of the holy Church of God is sup- [825] posed to portray), the Word leads the soul to the knowledge of the [CCSG 52] intelligible things that is immaterial, simple, unchanging, godlike, and free of all form and shape (as is indicated in the entrance of the ineffable mysteries). The soul then gathers to herself her proper powers and unites herself to the Word in the mind through the intel- [830] lectual kiss of peace, and the Word teaches the soul to confess with thanksgiving the ineffable principles and modes of her salvation through the symbol[173] of the faith.

Once these things have come to pass, the soul now finally encompasses[174] the principles of the sensible and intelligible things [835] in knowledge through instruction according to the simple and undivided power. After crossing over beyond all things,[175] the Word leads the soul to the knowledge of illustrious theology, providing an intelligence equal to the angels, in as far as it is possible for the soul. And the Word teaches the soul with such wisdom that it knows that "God is one," "one substance and three persons," a monad of [840] substance in three persons and a "triad" of persons "in the same substance,"[176] "a monad in triad and a triad in monad." God is not one and another, not one beside another, not one through another, not one in another, not one out of another; God, identically both monad and triad, is the same in himself, and according to himself, and with [845] himself. He possesses both a oneness that is without composition

---

[173]I.e., the Nicene-Constantinopolitan Creed.

[174]περιλαμβάνω; the word could also be translated "to grasp" or "embrace." The sense is that the soul now encompasses both of these realities and unites them in itself, thereby resulting in the soul's knowledge of these realities.

[175]Perhaps Maximus is referring to the soul encompassing all sensible and intelligible things.

[176]Justinian I, *Edictum Rectae Fidei* (p. 72, 1.12–13, 16, 22). The Greek for this citation is: μονάδα οὐσίας τρισυπόστατον καὶ τριάδα ὑποστάσεων ὁμοούσιον. This exceedingly technical phrase could also be translated: "a tri-hypostatic monad of essence and a co-essential triad of hypostases."

μονάδα μὲν κατὰ τὸν τῆς οὐσίας, ἤτοι <701a> τὸν τοῦ εἶναι λόγον, ἀλλ᾽ οὐ κατὰ σύνθεσιν ἢ συναίρεσιν ἢ τὴν οἱανοῦν σύγχυσιν, τριάδα δὲ κατὰ τὸν τοῦ πῶς ὑπάρχειν καὶ ὑφεστάναι λόγον, ἀλλ᾽ οὐ κατὰ διαίρεσιν ἢ ἀλλοτρίωσιν ἢ τὸν οἱονοῦν μερισμόν. οὐ γὰρ μεμέρισται ταῖς ὑποστάσεσιν ἡ μονάς, οὐδὲ σχετικῶς ἔνεστι καὶ ἐπιθεωρεῖται αὐταῖς, οὐδὲ συντέθεινται εἰς μονάδα αἱ ὑποστάσεις ἢ συναιρέσει αὐτὴν ἐκπληροῦσιν, ἀλλὰ τὴν αὐτὴν ἑαυτῇ ταυτόν, ἄλλως μέντοι καὶ ἄλλως. Μονὰς γάρ ἐστι ἀσύγχυτος τῇ οὐσίᾳ καὶ τῷ κατ᾽ αὐτὴν ἁπλῷ λόγῳ ἡ ἁγία Τριὰς τῶν ὑποστάσεων, καὶ τριάς ἐστι ταῖς ὑποστάσεσι καὶ τῷ τρόπῳ τῆς ὑπάρξεως ἡ ἁγία Μονάς. τὴν αὐτὴν ὅλην τοῦτο κἀκεῖνο διαφόρως, κατ᾽ ἄλλον καὶ ἄλλον, ὡς εἴρηται, λόγον νοουμένην· μίαν καὶ μόνην, ἀδιαίρετόν τε καὶ ἀσύγχυτον, καὶ <701b> ἁπλῆν καὶ ἀμείωτον καὶ ἀπαράλλακτον θεότητα· μονάδα κατὰ τὴν οὐσίαν ὅλην ὑπάρχουσαν, καὶ ὅλην τριάδα τὴν αὐτὴν ταῖς ὑποστάσεσι, καὶ μίαν ἑνὸς τρισσοφαοῦς ἀκτῖνα φωτὸς μονοειδῶς ἐπιλάμπουσαν.

Ἐφ᾽ ᾧ καὶ τὴν ψυχήν, ὁμοτίμως τοῖς ἁγίοις ἀγγέλοις τοὺς ἐκφανεῖς καὶ ἐφικτοὺς τῇ κτίσει περὶ θεότητος δεξαμένην λόγους καὶ συμφώνως αὐτοῖς ἀσιγήτως ἀνυμνεῖν μαθοῦσαν τριαδικῶς τὴν μίαν θεότητα, ἐπὶ τὴν κατὰ χάριν δι᾽ ὁμοιότητος ἐμφεροῦς υἱοθεσίαν ἀχθῆναι, δι᾽ ἧς μετ᾽ εὐχὰς τὸν Θεὸν Πατέρα μυστικόν τε χάριτι καὶ μόνον ἔχουσα πρὸς τὸ ἓν τῆς αὐτοῦ κρυφιότητος κατ᾽ ἔκστασιν πάντων συναχθήσεται, καὶ τοσοῦτον πείσεται μᾶλλον ἢ γνώσεται τὰ θεῖα, ὅσον μὴ ἑαυτῆς εἶναι βούλεσθαι, μηδὲ ἐξ ἑαυτῆς ὑφ᾽ ἑαυτῆς ἢ ἄλλου τινὸς <701c> γνωσθῆναι δύνασθαι, ἢ μόνου τοῦ ὅλην ἀγαθοπρεπῶς αὐτὴν ἀνειληφότος

and without confusion and a distinction that is undivided and [CCSG 53] inseparable. "On the one hand, he is a monad with reference to the word 'substance'"[177] but not according to composition, contraction, or any such of confusion. "And on the other hand, he is a triad with reference to" the words "existence" and "subsistence" but not [850] according to division, alienation, or any such separation. For the monad is not apportioned to the hypostases, nor is it in them relationally nor an aspect of them; neither are the hypostases composed into a monad, nor do they fulfill it by contraction. But God, who is identically monad and triad in himself, is perceived both in one manner and in another manner. For, the holy triad of persons is a [855] monad without confusion in substance and in the simplicity of his nature,[178] and the holy monad is a triad in persons and in the mode of his existence. The same whole is perceived variously according to one principle or another, as has been said above; the deity is one and unique, undivided and without confusion, simple, undiminished, [860] and invariable. The whole monad exists according to substance and the same whole triad exists in persons; one ray of one thrice-haloed light monadically shining forth.

In this light the soul receives the luminous principles concerning deity in a manner equal in degree to the holy angels and to [865] the extent that it is possible for a creature, and the soul learns to [CCSG 54] praise ceaselessly and triadically the one deity in harmony with the angels because the soul has been elevated to the adoption of sons and resembles his image by grace. Through adoption, because in prayer[179] the soul possesses God the Father mystically and by grace and uniquely, the soul will be gathered to the unity of his hiddenness by being separated from all things. And to the extent that the soul [870] "will experience" rather than know about "the divine things,"[180] the

---

[177]Justinian I, *Edictum Rectae Fidei* (p. 72, l.17–18).

[178]τῷ κατ' αὐτὴν ἁπλῷ λόγῳ: literally: "in the simple principle according to himself."

[179]Maximus teaches that the Lord's Prayer and the address of God as Father in the opening line speak to our adoption of sons.

[180]Pseudo-Dionysius, *On the Divine Names* 2.9.

ὅλου Θεοῦ, καὶ ὅλον αὐτῇ θεοπρεπῶς ὅλη [ὅλων αὐτῇ θεοπρεπῶς ὅλως][102] καὶ ἀπαθῶς ἑαυτὸν ἐνιέντος καὶ ὅλην θεοποιήσαντος·[103] ὡς εἶναι, καθώς φησιν ὁ πανάγιος Ἀρεοπαγίτης Διονύσιος, εἰκόνα καὶ φανέρωσιν τοῦ ἀφανοῦς φωτός, ἔσοπτρον ἀκραιφνές, διειδέστατον, ἀλώβητον, ἄχραντον, ἀκηλίδωτον, εἰσδεχόμενον ὅλην, εἰ θέμις εἰπεῖν, τὴν ὡραιότητα τοῦ ἀγαθοτύπου, θεοειδῶς[104] καὶ ἀμειώτως[105] ἐπιλάμπον ἐν ἑαυτῷ, καθάπερ οἷόν τέ ἐστι, τὴν ἀγαθότητα τῆς ἐν ἀδύτοις σιγῆς.

<701d> **Κεφαλ. ΚΔ. Τίνων ἐστὶν ἐνεργητική τε καὶ ἀποτελιστικὴ μυστηρίων, διὰ τῶν τελουμένων κατὰ τὴν ἁγίαν σύναξιν θεσμῶν ἐν τοῖς πιστοῖς καὶ πιστῶς συναγομένοις, ἡ παραμένουσα[106] τοῦ ἁγίου Πνεύματος χάρις**

Τοιγαροῦν ᾤετο δεῖν ὁ μακάριος γέρων καὶ παρακαλεῖν οὐκ ἐπαύετο πάντα Χριστιανὸν τῇ ἁγίᾳ τοῦ Θεοῦ Ἐκκλησίᾳ σχολάζειν καὶ μὴ ἀπολιμπάνεσθαί ποτε τῆς ἐν αὐτῇ τελουμένης ἁγίας συνάξεως, διά τε τοὺς παραμένοντας αὐτῇ ἁγίους ἀγγέλους, καὶ ἀπογραφομένους <704a> ἑκάστοτε τοὺς εἰσιόντας καὶ ἐμφανίζοντας τῷ Θεῷ καὶ τὰς ὑπὲρ αὐτῶν δεήσεις ποιουμένους, καὶ διὰ τὴν ἀοράτως ἀεὶ μὲν παροῦσαν τοῦ ἁγίου Πνεύματος χάριν, ἰδιοτρόπως δὲ μάλιστα κατὰ τὸν καιρὸν τῆς ἁγίας συνάξεως, καὶ ἕκαστον τῶν εὑρισκομένων μεταποιοῦσάν τε καὶ μετασκευάζουσαν, καὶ ἀληθὲς[107] μεταπλάττουσαν ἐπὶ τὸ θειότερον ἀναλόγως ἑαυτῷ, καὶ πρὸς τὸ δηλούμενον διὰ τῶν τελουμένων μυστηρίων ἄγουσαν·

[102]om. CCSG
[103]θεοποιήσαντος καὶ πρὸς ἑαυτὸν ἀμεταβόλους μεταποιήσαντος CCSG
[104]θεοειδείας CCSG
[105]ἀμιγῶς CCSG
[106]παραμένουσα τῇ ἐκκλησίᾳ CCSG
[107]ἀληθῶς CCSG

soul will neither desire to belong to herself nor will she be able to be known from herself, by herself, or by anyone else other than God alone. The whole of God will assume the whole soul in a way that is worthy of the good, and he will implant the whole of himself in the whole soul in a way that is worthy of God and without passion. He [875] will deify the whole soul and transform it unalterably into himself, so as "to be," as the all-holy Dionysius the Areopagite says, "an image and manifestation of the unseen light, a mirror, pure, bright, untarnished, unspotted, receiving, if one may so, the whole loveliness of [880] the divine goodness and purely enlightening within itself as far as [CCSG 55] possible the goodness of silence in the inner sanctuaries."[181]

[24] What are the Mysteries that the Grace of the Holy Spirit Who Abides in the Church Effects and Perfects through the Ordinances Performed in the Holy Synaxis among Those Who Are Faithful and Faithfully Assembled

For this reason, the blessed elder believed—and he never ceased to exhort us—that it is necessary for every Christian to attend the holy Church of God and never to be absent from the holy synaxis that is [885] performed in the Church. He believed this firstly[182] because of the holy angels who abide in the Church, who register those who enter each assembly and report to God, and who offer intercessory prayers on their behalf. He believed this secondly because of the grace of the Holy Spirit that is always invisibly present but is present in a [890] special way during the time of the holy synaxis. This grace remakes, reshapes—and to speak truly—transforms each one found there into [CCSG 56] something more divine in a way that is proportionate to him. And this grace leads each one to that which is signified by the mysteries

---

[181]Ibid., *Div. Nom* 4.22.

[182]Chapter 24 is a single sentence in Greek (from lines 883 until 935). The impossibility of translating these pages as a single sentence in English made it necessary for the translators to structure Maximus' thought as several English sentences, and some restatement of subjects and objects of the sentence has been necessary. It is in instances such as these that translators lament that the poetry and logical pattern of the original text cannot be exactly reproduced in translation.

κἂν αὐτὸς μὴ αἰσθάνηται, εἴπερ τῶν ἔτι κατὰ Χριστὸν νηπίων ἐστὶ καὶ εἰς τὸ βάθος τῶν γινομένων ὁρᾶν ἀδυνατεῖ, καὶ τὴν δηλουμένην δι᾽ ἑκάστου τῶν τελουμένων θείων συμβόλων τῆς σωτηρίας ἐν αὐτῷ χάριν ἐνεργοῦσαν, καθ᾽ εἱρμὸν καὶ τάξιν ἀπὸ τῶν προσεχῶν μέχρι τοῦ πάντων τέλους ὁδεύουσαν.[108]

<704b> Κατὰ μὲν πρώτην εἴσοδον ἀπιστίας ἀποβολήν, πίστεως αὔξησιν, κακίας μείωσιν, ἀρετῆς ἐπίδοσιν, ἀγνοίας ἀφανισμόν, γνώσεως προσθήκην.[109]

Διὰ δὲ τῆς ἀκροάσεως τῶν θείων λογίων τὰς τῶν εἰρημένων τούτων, πίστεώς φημι καὶ ἀρετῆς καὶ γνώσεως, παγίας καὶ ἀμεταθέτους ἕξεις τε καὶ διαθέσεις.[110]

Διὰ δὲ τῶν ἐπὶ τούτοις θείων ἀσμάτων τὴν πρὸς τὰς ἀρετὰς τῆς ψυχῆς ἑκούσιον συγκατάθεσιν καὶ τὴν ἐπ᾽ αὐταῖς ἐγγινομένην αὐτῇ νοερὰν ἡδονὴν καὶ τερπνότητα.[111]

Διὰ δὲ τῆς ἱερᾶς ἀναγνώσεως τοῦ ἁγίου Εὐαγγελίου τὴν τοῦ χοϊκοῦ φρονήματος, ὥσπερ αἰσθητοῦ κόσμου, συντέλειαν.[112]

Διὰ δὲ τῆς μετὰ ταῦτα τῶν θυρῶν κλείσεως τὴν κατὰ διάθεσιν ἀπὸ τούτου τοῦ φθαρτοῦ κόσμου πρὸς τὸν νοητὸν κόσμον

---

[108]περὶ τῆς πρώτης εἰσόδου add. CCSG
[109]περὶ τῶν ἀναγνωσμάτων add. CCSG
[110]περὶ τῶν ᾀσμάτων add. CCSG
[111]περὶ τοῦ ἁγίου εὐαγγελίου add. CCSG
[112]περὶ τῆς κλείσεως τῶν θυρῶν add. CCSG

performed during the holy synaxis, even if he does not perceive it with his senses because he is still an "infant in Christ"[183] and he is [895] unable to see into the depth of what is occurring. And this grace is signified by each of the divine symbols of salvation performed and at the same time is also at work in each one, proceeding in sequence and order from that which follows until the end of all things:

Concerning the First Entrance:

In the first entrance, grace brings about the rejection of unbelief, the [900] growth of faith, the diminishment of evil, the advancement in virtue, the vanishing of ignorance, and the addition of knowledge.

Concerning the Readings:

Through the hearing of the divine oracles, grace brings about the steadfast and immutable habits and dispositions of the things that have been mentioned above—I am speaking of faith, virtue, and [905] knowledge.

Concerning the Songs:

Through the divine songs added to the readings, grace brings about voluntary assent to the virtues of the soul and the intellectual pleasure and delight that spring up in the soul because of these virtues.

Concerning the Holy Gospel: [CCSG 57]

Through the sacred reading of the holy Gospel, grace brings about the end of the earthly mindset, as the end of the sensible realm. [910]

Concerning the Closing of the Doors:

Through the closing of the doors after these things, grace brings about the passing on and transposition of the soul according to

[183] 1 Cor 3.1.

μετάβασιν τῆς ψυχῆς <704c> καὶ μετάθεσιν, δι' ἧς τὰς αἰσθήσεις θυρῶν δίκην μύσασα, τῶν καθ' ἁμαρτίαν εἰδώλων καθαρὰς ἀπεργάζεται.[113]

Διὰ δὲ τῆς εἰσόδου τῶν ἁγίων μυστηρίων τὴν τελειωτέραν καὶ μυστικωτέραν καὶ καινὴν περὶ τὴν[114] εἰς ἡμᾶς οἰκονομίαν[115] τοῦ Θεοῦ διδασκαλίαν καὶ γνῶσιν.[116]

Διὰ δὲ τοῦ θείου ἀσπασμοῦ τὴν πάντων πρὸς πάντας καὶ πρὸς ἑαυτὸν ἑκάστου πρότερον καὶ τὸν Θεὸν ὁμονοίας καὶ ὁμογνωμοσύνης καὶ ἀγάπης ταυτότητα.[117]

Διὰ δὲ τῆς τοῦ Συμβόλου τῆς πίστεως ὁμολογίας τὴν ἐπὶ τοῖς παραδόξοις τρόποις τῆς σωτηρίας ἡμῶν πρόσφορον εὐχαριστίαν.[118]

Διὰ δὲ τοῦ Τρισαγίου τὴν πρὸς τοὺς ἁγίους ἀγγέλους ἕνωσίν τε καὶ ἰσοτιμίαν καὶ τὴν ἄπαυστον τῆς ἁγιαστικῆς δοξολογίας τοῦ Θεοῦ σύμφωνον εὐτονίαν.[119]

Διὰ δὲ τῆς <704d> προσευχῆς, δι' ἧς Πατέρα καλεῖν τὸν Θεὸν ἀξιούμεθα, τὴν ἐν χάριτι τοῦ ἁγίου Πνεύματος ἀληθεστάτην υἱοθεσίαν.[120]

---

[113]περὶ τῆς εἰσόδου τῶν ἁγίων add. CCSG
[114]τῆς CCSG
[115]οἰκονομίας CCSG
[116]περὶ τοῦ ἀσπασμοῦ add. CCSG
[117]περὶ τοῦ συμβόλου add. CCSG
[118]περὶ τοῦ τρισαγίου add. CCSG
[119]περὶ τοῦ Πάτερ ἡμῶν add. CCSG
[120]περὶ τοῦ Εἷς ἅγιος καῖ τῶν ἑξῆς add. CCSG

her disposition from this perishable realm to the intelligible realm, whereby is completed the shutting of the senses like doors and the cleansing of the senses from the idols of sin.   [915]

Concerning the Entrance of the Holy Mysteries:

Through the entrance of the holy mysteries, grace brings about the more perfect and more mystical and new teaching and knowledge concerning God's dispensation toward us.

Concerning the Kiss of Peace:

Through the divine kiss of peace, grace brings about the identity of unanimity, agreement, and love of everyone toward everyone and of   [920] each one toward himself and foremost toward God.

Concerning the Symbol:[184]   [CCSG 58]

Through the confession of the symbol of the faith, grace brings about a suitable thankfulness for the miraculous ways of our salvation.

Concerning the Trisagion:

Through the Trisagion, grace brings about oneness with the angels,   [925] and equality of honor, and the endless, harmonious pitch[185] of the doxology ascribing sanctity to God.

Concerning the Our Father:

Through the prayer in which we are deemed worthy to call God "Father," the truest adoption is brought about by the grace of the Holy Spirit.

---

[184]I.e., the Nicene-Constantinopolitan Creed.

[185]εὐτονία; this word carries the connotation of being "well-strung," like a musical instrument.

Διὰ δὲ τοῦ Εἷς ἅγιος καὶ τῶν ἑξῆς τὴν πρὸς αὐτὸν τὸν Θεὸν
ἑνοποιὸν χάριν καὶ οἰκειότητα.¹²¹

Διὰ δὲ τῆς ἁγίας μεταλήψεως τῶν ἀχράντων καὶ ζωοποιῶν
μυστηρίων τὴν πρὸς αὐτὸν κατὰ μέθεξιν ἐνδεχομένην δι᾽
ὁμοιότητος κοινωνίαν τε καὶ ταυτότητα, δι᾽ ἧς γενέσθαι θεὸς ἐξ
ἀνθρώπου καταξιοῦται ὁ ἄνθρωπος.

Ὧν γὰρ ἐνταῦθα κατὰ τὴν παροῦσαν ζωὴν διὰ τῆς ἐν πίστει
χάριτος πιστεύομεν μετειληφέναι δωρεῶν τοῦ ἁγίου Πνεύματος,
τούτων ἐν τῷ μέλλοντι αἰῶνι κατὰ ἀλήθειαν ἀνυποστάτως¹²²
αὐτῷ τῷ πράγματι κατὰ τὴν ἄπτωτον ἐλπίδα τῆς πίστεως ἡμῶν
καὶ τὴν τοῦ ἐπαγγειλομένου <705a> βεβαίαν καὶ ἀπαράβατον
ὑπόσχεσιν, φυλάξαντες κατὰ δύναμιν τὰς ἐντολὰς πιστεύομεν
καταλήψεσθαι,¹²³ μεταβαίνοντες ἀπὸ τῆς ἐν πίστει χάριτος εἰς
τὴν κατ᾽ εἶδος χάριν, μεταποιοῦντος ἡμᾶς πρὸς ἑαυτὸν δηλαδὴ
τοῦ Θεοῦ καὶ Σωτῆρος ἡμῶν Ἰησοῦ Χριστοῦ, τῇ περιαιρέσει τῶν
ἐν ἡμῖν τῆς φθορᾶς γνωρισμάτων, καὶ τὰ παραδειχθέντα διὰ
τῶν ἐνταῦθα αἰσθητῶν συμβόλων ἡμῖν ἀρχέτυπα χαριζομένου
μυστήρια.¹²⁴

Διὰ δὲ τὸ εὐμνημόνευτον, εἰ δοκεῖ, τὴν τῶν εἰρημένων δύναμιν
κατ᾽ ἐπιτομὴν ἐπιδραμόντες, οὕτω κεφαλαιώσωμεν.

¹²¹περὶ τῆς μεταλήψεος add. CCSG
¹²²ἐνυποστάτως CCSG
¹²³μεταλήψεσθαι CCSG
¹²⁴ἀνακεφαλαίωσις add. CCSG

Concerning the "One is Holy" and the Hymns that Follow

Through the "One is Holy" and the hymns that follow, we experience [930] the grace and intimacy that unites us with God himself.

Concerning the Partaking

Through the holy partaking of the immaculate and life-giving mysteries, grace brings about the fellowship and identity with God according to participation that is possible through our likeness to God, and through this identity man is deemed worthy to become [935] god from man.

For, we believe that we have partaken of the gifts of the Holy [CCSG 59] Spirit through grace by faith here in this present life, and we believe that, after keeping the commandments to the best of our ability, we shall partake in these things in their very reality—in the age to come according to that which is ultimately true,[186] according to the unfail- [940] ing hope of our faith and the certain and infallible fulfillment of what has been promised. As we pass from the grace that is by faith to the grace according to sight, he will remake us into himself—clearly, I am speaking of "our God and Savior Jesus Christ"[187]—by stripping away the properties of corruption in us, and he will graciously give [945] to us the archetypal mysteries that are represented here through sensible symbols.

Summary

"For ease of remembering, let us sum up,"[188] if you please, revisiting in summary form the most important parts of what has been said above.

---

[186]ἐνυποστάτως: this term can also mean "substantially" or "personally" in the context of Trinitarian theology. Thus, Maximus may also mean that we will experience these things "according to the truth in the manner of God's own person."

[187]Tit 2.13. In the Greek, "he will remake" [μεταποιοῦντος] is not a finite verb, and Maximus' identification of the subject as "our God and Savior Jesus Christ" is not only a theological statement but also a helpful grammatical clarification.

[188]Gregory of Nazianzus, *Oration* 30.1.

Ἔστι μὲν οὖν ἡ ἁγία Ἐκκλησία τύπος, ὡς εἴρηται, καὶ εἰκὼν τοῦ μὲν Θεοῦ, διότι ἥν ἐργάζεται κατὰ τὴν ἄπειρον αὐτοῦ δύναμιν καὶ <705b> σοφίαν περὶ τὰς διαφόρους τῶν ὄντων οὐσίας ἀσύγχυτον ἔνωσιν, ὡς δημιουργὸς κατ' ἄκρον ἑαυτῷ συνέχων καὶ[125] κατὰ μίαν τῆς πίστεως καὶ χάριν καὶ κλῆσιν τοὺς πιστοὺς ἀλλήλοις ἑνοειδῶς συνάπτουσα, τοὺς δὲ πρακτικοὺς καὶ ἐναρέτους, κατὰ μίαν γνώμης ταυτότητα, τοὺς δὲ θεωρητικοὺς καὶ γνωστικοὺς πρὸς τούτοις καὶ καθ' ὁμόνοιαν ἀρραγῆ καὶ ἀδιαίρετον.

Τοῦ δὲ κόσμου, τοῦ τε νοητοῦ καὶ τοῦ αἰσθητοῦ τύπος ἐστίν, ὡς τοῦ νοητοῦ κόσμου τὸ ἱερατεῖον σύμβολον ἔχουσα, τοῦ αἰσθητοῦ δέ, τὸν ναόν.

<705c> Ἀνθρώπου δὲ πάλιν εἰκών ἐστιν, ὡς τὴν ψυχὴν διὰ τοῦ ἱερατείου μιμουμένη, τὸ δὲ σῶμα διὰ τοῦ ναοῦ προβαλλομένη.

Αὐτῆς δὲ τῆς ψυχῆς καθ' ἑαυτὴν νοουμένης τύπος ἐστὶ καὶ εἰκών, ὡς τοῦ θεωρητικοῦ διὰ τοῦ ἱερατείου φέρουσα τὸ ἐπίδοξον, τοῦ δὲ πρακτικοῦ διὰ τοῦ ναοῦ τὸ κόσμιον ἔχουσα.

Τῆς δὲ τελουμένης ἐν αὐτῇ ἁγίας συνάξεως ἡ μὲν πρώτη εἴσοδος γενικῶς μὲν δηλοῖ τὴν πρώτην τοῦ Θεοῦ ἡμῶν παρουσίαν, ἰδικῶς δὲ τὴν δι' αὐτοῦ καὶ σὺν αὐτῷ τῶν ἐξ ἀπιστίας εἰς πίστιν καὶ ἀπὸ κακίας εἰς ἀρετὴν καὶ ἀπὸ ἀγνωσίας εἰς γνῶσιν εἰσαγομένων ἐπιστροφήν.

<705d> Τὰ δὲ γινόμενα μετ' αὐτὴν ἀναγνώσματα γενικῶς μὲν τὰ θεῖα θελήματά τε καὶ βουλήματα, καθ' ἃ χρὴ τοὺς πάντας

---

[125] καὶ αὐτὴ CCSG

Therefore, the holy Church is a representation and image of God, [950] as it has been said above, because the unconfused oneness, which she works according to God's boundless power and wisdom from the [CCSG 60] different substances of the things that exist, God works as Creator and who holds all things together by holding all things to himself as their summit.[189] And the Church works this oneness in the faithful according to the grace of faith—on the one hand, she joins all the faithful to one another in unity according to the one grace and [955] calling of faith; on the other hand, she joins the practical and the contemplative ones according to the one identity of their intention, and the virtuous and the enlightened ones according to an unbroken and undivided unanimity.

The Church is a representation of the intelligible and sensible [960] realms, because she possesses the sanctuary as a symbol of the intelligible realm and the nave as a symbol of the sensible realm.

And, she is also an image of man, because she portrays the soul through the sanctuary, and she presents the body through the nave.

She is a representation and image of the soul considered on [965] its own, because she bears the eminence of the contemplative part through the sanctuary, and she possesses the ornamentation of the practical part through the nave.

The first entrance of the holy synaxis that is performed in the Church indicates the first coming of Christ our God in a universal sense. But, in an individual sense, it indicates the conversion of those [970] who through him and with him are brought from unbelief into faith, and from evil into virtue, and from ignorance into knowledge.

The readings that come after this reveal in a universal sense the divine will[190] and purposes according to which everyone ought to

---

[189]ὡς δημιουργὸς κατ᾽ ἄκρον ἑαυτῷ συνέχων; this phrase is notably briefer in Greek.

[190]βουλήματα; the word translated "will" above is in fact in the plural in Greek. Although not the principal term debated during the Monothelite controversy (θέλημα), nevertheless Maximus' use of the plural may reflect his dyothelitism.

παιδεύεσθαί τε καὶ πολιτεύεσθαι, μηνύει· ἰδικῶς δὲ τὴν κατὰ τὴν πίστιν διδασκαλίαν καὶ προκοπὴν τῶν πιστευσάντων, καὶ τῶν πρακτικῶν τὴν κατ᾽ ἀρετὴν παγίαν διάθεσιν, καθ᾽ ἣν τῷ θείῳ νόμῳ στοιχοῦντες τῶν ἐντολῶν ἀνδρικῶς τε καὶ ἀκλονήτως ἵστανται πρὸς τὰς μεθοδείας τοῦ διαβόλου, καὶ τὰς ἀντικειμένας ἐνεργείας διαδιδράσκουσι, καὶ τῶν γνωστικῶν τὴν κατὰ θεωρίαν ἕξιν, καθ᾽ ἣν τοὺς τῶν αἰσθητῶν καὶ τῆς ἐπ᾽ αὐτοῖς προνοίας <708a> πνευματικοὺς κατὰ δύναμιν συλλεγόμενοι λόγους, ἀπλανῶς πρὸς τὴν ἀλήθειαν φέρονται.

Τὰ δὲ θεῖα τῶν ᾀσμάτων μελίσματα τὴν ἐγγινομένην ταῖς ἁπάντων ψυχαῖς θείαν ἡδονὴν καὶ τερπνότητα, καθ᾽ ἣν μυστικῶς ῥωννύμεναι τῶν μὲν παρελθόντων τῆς ἀρετῆς ἐπιλανθάνονται πόνων, πρὸς δὲ τὴν τῶν λειπομένων θείων καὶ ἀκηράτων ἀγαθῶν νεάζουσι εὔτονον ἔφεσιν.

Τὸ δὲ ἅγιον Εὐαγγέλιον γενικῶς μὲν σύμβολόν ἐστι τῆς συντελείας τοῦ αἰῶνος τούτου, ἰδικῶς δὲ τῶν μὲν πιστευσάντων δηλοῖ τὸν παντελῆ τῆς ἀρχαίας πλάνης ἀφανισμόν, τῶν δὲ πρακτικῶν τὴν νέκρωσιν καὶ συντέλειαν τοῦ κατὰ σάρκα νόμου τε <708b> καὶ φρονήματος, τῶν δὲ γνωστικῶν τὴν πρὸς τὸν συνεκτικώτατον λόγον τῶν πολλῶν καὶ διαφόρων λόγων συναγωγήν τε καὶ ἀναφοράν, συντελεσθείσης αὐτοῖς καὶ περατωθείσης τῆς διεξοδικωτέρας καὶ ποικιλοτέρας φυσικῆς θεωρίας.

Ἡ δὲ τοῦ ἀρχιερέως ἀπὸ τοῦ θρόνου κατάβασις καὶ ἡ τῶν κατηχουμένων ἐκβολὴ γενικῶς μὲν σημαίνει τὴν ἀπ᾽ οὐρανοῦ[126]

---

[126] οὐρανῶν CCSG

be instructed and conduct himself.[191] But, in an individual sense, [975; they reveal the teaching in faith, the progress of those who believe, CCSG 61] and the steadfast disposition in the virtues of the practical ones, by which those who keep in step[192] with the divine law of the commandments courageously and unswervingly "stand against the wiles of the devil"[193] and escape his adversarial activity. The readings also [980] reveal the habit in contemplation of the enlightened ones, and by this contemplation those who search to the best of their ability for the spiritual principles of the sensible things and of the providential care that they receive are unerringly brought to the truth.

The divine melodies of the songs indicate the divine pleasure and delight that spring up in the souls of the people. And when they [985] have been mystically strengthened, they forget their past sufferings for virtue and feel a youthful and vigorous[194] desire for the divine and undefiled blessings that they have yet to attain.

In a universal sense, the holy Gospel is a symbol of the end of this [990] age. But, in an individual sense, it indicates the complete vanishing of the primordial error for those who believe. For the practical ones, it indicates the deadness and end of the law and mindset that are according to the flesh; for the enlightened ones, who have completed detailed and difficult courses of study in natural contemplation, it indicates the [995] attraction to and the reference back to the principle that holds together all things on the part of the many and different principles.

The descent of the high-priest from the throne and the dismissal [CCSG 62] of the catechumens signifies, in a universal sense, the second coming from heaven "of our great God and Savior Jesus Christ,"[195] the [1000]

---

[191]πολιτεύω; this term can also mean "to be a citizen." Maximus is specifically referring to conducting one's life in a manner appropriate for a citizen of the kingdom of heaven.

[192]στοιχέω; this term has a rich array of meanings in Pauline literature, all of which speak to the transmission of orthodoxy; see Rom 4.12, Gal 5.25, 6.16, Phil 3.16.

[193]Eph 6.11.

[194]εὔτονος; the word can be a musical term, referring to a string pulled tight on an instrument.

[195]Tit 2.13.

δευτέραν τοῦ μεγάλου Θεοῦ καὶ Σωτῆρος ἡμῶν Ἰησοῦ Χριστοῦ
παρουσίαν καὶ τὸν ἀπὸ τῶν ἁγίων ἀφορισμὸν τῶν ἁμαρτωλῶν
καὶ τὴν δικαίαν πρὸς τὴν ἑκάστου ἀξίαν ἀμοιβήν, ἰδικῶς δέ, τὴν
τελείαν ἐν πίστει τῶν πιστευσάντων <708c> πληροφορίαν, ἣν ποιεῖ
παραγινόμενος[127] ἀοράτως ὁ Θεὸς καὶ Λόγος, δι' ἧς πᾶς ἔτι καθ'
ὁτιοῦν σκάζων κατὰ τὴν πίστιν λογισμός, κατηχουμένου τρόπον,
αὐτῶν ἀπελαύνεται· τῶν δὲ πρακτικῶν τὴν τελείαν ἀπάθειαν, δι' ἧς
πᾶς ἐμπαθὴς καὶ ἀφώτιστος λογισμὸς τῆς ψυχῆς ἀπογίνεται· τῶν
δὲ γνωστικῶν τὴν συνεκτικὴν ἐπιστήμην τῶν ἐπεγνωσμένων,[128]
δι' ἧς πᾶσαι τῶν ὑλικῶν αἱ εἰκόνες τῆς ψυχῆς ἐκδιώκονται.

Ἡ δὲ κλεῖσις τῶν θυρῶν, καὶ ἡ τῶν ἁγίων Μυστηρίων εἴσοδος
καὶ ὁ θεῖος ἀσπασμὸς καὶ ἡ τοῦ Συμβόλου τῆς πίστεως ἐκφώνησις,
γενικῶς μὲν δηλοῖ τὴν τῶν αἰσθητῶν πάροδον καὶ τὴν τῶν
νοητῶν φανέρωσιν, καὶ τὴν καινὴν τοῦ περὶ ἡμᾶς θείου <708d>
μυστηρίου διδαχήν, καὶ τὴν πρὸς πάντας πάντων ἑαυτούς τε
καὶ τὸν Θεὸν γενησομένην ὁμονοίας[129] καὶ ὁμογνωμοσύνης[130]
καὶ ἀγάπης[131] ταυτότητα, καὶ τὴν ἐφ' οἷς ἐσώθημεν τρόποις
εὐχαριστίαν· ἰδικῶς δὲ τῶν μὲν πιστῶν τὴν ἀπὸ τῆς πλάνης[132]
πίστεως εἰς τὴν ἐν δόγμασι διδαχὴν καὶ μύησιν καὶ ὁμοφωνίαν καὶ
εὐσέβειαν προκοπήν. τὸ γὰρ πρῶτον ἡ τῶν θυρῶν δηλοῖ κλεῖσις,
τὸ δεύτερον δὲ ἡ τῶν ἁγίων εἴσοδος, τὸ δὲ τρίτον ὁ ἀσπασμός, καὶ
τὸ τέταρτον ἡ ἐκφώνησις τοῦ σοβόλου·[133] τῶν δὲ πρακτικῶν, τὴν
ἀπὸ πράξεως εἰς θεωρίαν μυσάντων τὰς αἰσθήσεις καὶ ἔξω σαρκὸς
καὶ κόσμου γενομένων διὰ τῆς ἀποβολῆς τῶν <709a> κατ' αὐτὰς
ἐνεργειῶν μετάθεσιν, καὶ τὴν ἀπὸ τοῦ τρόπου τῶν ἐντολῶν εἰς τὸν
λόγον αὐτῶν ἀνάβασιν, καὶ τὴν αὐτῶν τῶν ἐντολῶν κατὰ τοὺς
οἰκείους λόγους συγγενῆ πρὸς τὰς δυνάμεις τῆς ψυχῆς οἰκειότητά

---

[127]παραγινόμενος αὐτοῖς CCSG
[128]ἐγνωσμένων CCSG
[129]ὁμονοίαν CCSG
[130]ὁμογνωμοσύνην CCSG
[131]ἀγάπην καὶ CCSG
[132]ἁπλῆς CCSG
[133]Συμβόλου CCSG

separation of the sinners from the saints, and the just reward that is due to each one. But, in an individual sense, it signifies the complete assurance that those who believe possess by faith, because God the Word, who is invisibly present with them, grants this assurance. By this assurance, every thought that in some way still proceeds unsteadily regarding the faith is expelled from among the believers, as a catechumen is dismissed from the service. For the practical ones, [1005] it signifies the complete impassibility by which every passible and unilluminated thought departs from the soul. For the enlightened ones, it signifies the knowledge that holds together everything that has been known, by which all images of material things are banished from the soul.

The closing of the doors, the entrance of the holy mysteries, the [1010] divine kiss of peace, and the pronouncement of the symbol of the faith, indicate, in a universal sense, the passing away of the sensible things, the appearance of the intelligible things, the new teaching concerning the divine mystery in relation to us, the unanimity and agreement and love and identity of everyone with everyone and [1015] with God that will be, and the thanksgiving for the ways salvation [CCSG 63] has come to us. But, in an individual sense, they indicate the progress of the faithful from simple faith to teaching and initiation and unison and godliness in doctrine. (The closing of the doors indicates the first, the entrance of the saints the second, the kiss of peace the [1020] third, and the pronouncement of the symbol the fourth.) For the practical ones, "who shut out the senses and are outside the flesh and the world,"[196] they indicate the transposition from practice to contemplation through the rejection of the activities according to the senses, and the ascent from the mode of the commandments to [1025] their principle, and the intimacy and oneness that the commandments themselves possess with the powers of the soul by kinship according to their corresponding principles, and the habit that is apt to give thanks to God.[197] For the enlightened ones, they indicate the

---

[196]Gregory of Nazianzus, *Oration* 2.7.
[197]θεολογικὴν εὐχαριστίαν; literally: "theological thanksgiving."

τε καὶ ἕνωσιν, καὶ τὴν πρὸς θεολογικὴν εὐχαριστίαν ἐπιτήδειον ἕξιν· τῶν δὲ γνωστικῶν τὴν ἀπὸ τῆς φυσικῆς θεωρίας εἰς τὴν τῶν νοητῶν ἁπλῆν κατανόησιν, καθ᾽ ἣν οὐδαμῶς δι᾽ αἰσθήσεως ἤ τινος τῶν φαινομένων ἔτι τὸν θεῖον καὶ ἄρρητον μεταδιώκουσι λόγον, καὶ τὴν πρὸς τὴν ψυχὴν τῶν αὐτῆς δυνάμεων ἕνωσιν, καὶ τὴν κατὰ νοῦν ἑνοειδῶς συλλαμβάνουσαν τὸν τῆς[134] προνοίας λόγον ἁπλότητα.

<709b> Ἡ δὲ τοῦ Τρισαγίου ἄπαυστος τῶν ἁγίων ἀγγέλων ἁγιαστικὴ δοξολογία γενικῶς μὲν σημαίνει τὴν ἅμα τε καὶ ἐν ταὐτῷ γενησομένην κατὰ τὸν αἰῶνα τὸν μέλλοντα τῶν οὐρανίων καὶ ἐπιγείων δυνάμεων ἴσην καὶ πολιτείαν καὶ ἀγωγὴν καὶ συμφωνίαν τῆς θείας δοξολογίας, ἀθανατισθέντος τοῖς ἀνθρώποις τοῦ σώματος διὰ τῆς ἀναστάσεως καὶ μηκέτι βαροῦντος τὴν ψυχὴν τῇ φθορᾷ καὶ βαρουμένου, ἀλλὰ διὰ τῆς εἰς ἀφθαρσίαν ἀλλαγῆς πρὸς ὑποδοχὴν παρουσίας Θεοῦ λαβόντος καὶ δύναμιν καὶ ἐπιτηδειότητα· ἰδικῶς δὲ τῶν μὲν πιστῶν τὴν πρὸς ἀγγέλους κατὰ τὴν πίστιν θεολογικὴν ἅμιλλαν, τῶν δὲ πρακτικῶν τὴν ἰσάγγελον, ὡς ἐφικτὸν ἀνθρώποις, κατὰ τὸν βίον λαμπρότητα καὶ τὴν εὐτονίαν τῆς θεολογικῆς ὑμνολογίας, τῶν δὲ γνωστικῶν τὰς ἰσαγγέλους κατὰ <709c> τὸ δυνατὸν ἀνθρώποις περὶ θεότητος νοήσεις τε καὶ ὑμνήσεις καὶ ἀεικινησίας.

Ἡ δὲ μακαρία τοῦ μεγάλου Θεοῦ καὶ Πατρὸς ἐπίκλησις καὶ ἡ τοῦ Εἷς ἅγιος καὶ τῶν ἑξῆς ἐκφώνησις καὶ ἡ τῶν ἁγίων καὶ ζωοποιῶν μυστηρίων μετάληψις, τὴν ἐπὶ πᾶσι καὶ ἐπὶ πάντων τῶν ἀξίων ἐσομένην διὰ τὴν ἀγαθότητα τοῦ Θεοῦ ὑμῶν υἱοθεσίαν, ἕνωσίν τε καὶ οἰκειότητα καὶ ὁμοιότητα θείαν καὶ θέωσιν δηλοῖ· δι᾽ ἧς πάντα ἐν πᾶσιν ἔσται τοῖς σωζομένοις αὐτὸς ὁ Θεὸς ὁμοίως, ὡς κάλλος ἀρχέτυπον κατ᾽ αἰτίαν ἐμπρέπων τοῖς αὐτῷ δι᾽ ἀρετῆς καὶ γνώσεως κατὰ χάριν ὁμοίως συμπρέπουσι.

---

[134]τῆς θείας CCSG

transposition from natural contemplation to simple consideration of the intelligible things (and the enlightened ones pursue after the [1030] divine and ineffable principle through this simple consideration rather than any longer through sense perception or anything that [CCSG 64] appears), and the oneness that the soul possesses with her own powers, and the simplicity that comprehends the principle of divine providence in unity according to the mind.

The doxology of the holy angels ascribing holiness to God in the unceasing Trisagion signifies, in a universal sense, the future equal- [1035] ity in citizenship and conduct and harmony in the divine doxology that the heavenly and earthly powers will enjoy in this age and also in the age to come, when the human body will become immortal through the resurrection and no longer will burden the soul nor will [1040] be burdened by corruption. But, through the exchange for incorruptibility, the body will receive power and aptitude to welcome the presence of God. But, in an individual sense, for the faithful, it signifies the theological contest with the angels for the faith. For the practical ones, it signifies the splendor and pitch of the singing of hymns to God that is equal to the angels, in as far as this is possible [1045] for men in this life.[198] For the enlightened ones, it signifies the intelligence and praise and ceaseless motion that is equal to the angels, in as far men are able to possess these things concerning deity.

And the blessed invocation of our great God and Father, and the exclamation of the "One is Holy" and the hymns that follow, and the partaking of the saints even of the life-giving mysteries indicate [1050] the adoption—that is, the oneness, intimacy, divine likeness, and [CCSG 65] theosis—that will be to all and on all who are worthy on account of the goodness of our God. And through theosis, "God" himself "will be everything to everyone"[199] who is being saved, to those who are like him as beauty befits its archetypical cause, to those who likewise [1055] accord with him by grace through virtue and knowledge.

---

[198]θεολογικῆς ὑμνολογίας; literally: "theological singing of hymns."
[199]1 Cor 15.28.

<709d> Πιστοὺς δὲ καὶ ἐναρέτους καὶ γνωστικοὺς ἐκάλει τοὺς εἰσαγομένους καὶ τοὺς προκόπτοντας καὶ τοὺς τελείους, ἤγουν δούλους καὶ μισθίους καὶ υἱούς, τὰς τρεῖς τάξεις τῶν σωζομένων. δοῦλοι γάρ εἰσι πιστοί, οἱ φόβῳ τῶν ἠπειλημένων ἐκπληροῦντες τοῦ δεσπότου τὰς ἐντολὰς καὶ τοῖς πιστευθεῖσιν εὐνοϊκῶς ἐπεργαζόμενοι· μίσθιοι δὲ οἱ πόθῳ τῶν ἐπηγγελμένων ἀγαθῶν βαστάζοντες μεθ᾽ ὑπομονῆς τὸ βάρος τῆς ἡμέρας καὶ τὸν καύσονα,[135] τουτέστι τὴν ἔμφυτον καὶ συνεζευγμένην τῇ παρούσῃ ζωῇ ἐκ τῆς προπατορικῆς καταδίκης θλίψιν καὶ τοὺς ἐπ᾽ αὐτῇ ὑπὲρ <712a> τῆς ἀρετῆς πειρασμούς, καὶ ζωῆς ζωὴν σοφῶς κατ᾽ αὐθαίρετον γνώμην ἀνταλλάσσοντες, τῆς παρούσης τὴν μέλλουσαν· υἱοὶ δὲ οἱ μήτε φόβῳ τῶν ἠπειλημένων, μήτε πόθῳ τῶν ἐπηγγελμένων, ἀλλὰ τρόπῳ καὶ ἕξει τῆς πρὸς τὸ καλὸν κατὰ γνώμην τῆς ψυχῆς ῥοπῆς τε καὶ διαθέσεως μηδέποτε τοῦ Θεοῦ χωριζόμενοι κατ᾽ ἐκεῖνον τὸν υἱόν, πρὸς ὃν εἴρηται τέκνον, σὺ πάντοτε μετ᾽ ἐμοῦ εἶ, καὶ τὰ ἐμὰ πάντα σά ἐστι, τοῦτο κατὰ τὴν ἐν χάριτι θέσιν ἐνδεχομένως ὑπάρχοντες, ὅπερ ὁ Θεὸς κατὰ τὴν φύσιν καὶ αἰτίαν καὶ ἔστι καὶ πιστεύεται.

Μὴ τοίνυν ἀπολειφθῶμεν τῆς ἁγίας τοῦ Θεοῦ Ἐκκλησίας, τοσαῦτα κατὰ τὴν τῶν τελουμένων θείων <712b> συμβόλων ἁγίαν διάταξιν τῆς σωτηρίας ἡμῶν περιεχούσης μυστήρια, δι᾽ ὧν ἕκαστον ἡμῶν καλῶς μάλιστα πολιτευόμενον ἀναλόγως ἑαυτῷ κατὰ Χριστὸν δημιουργοῦσα τὸ δοθὲν διὰ τοῦ ἁγίου βαπτίσματος ἐν Πνεύματι ἁγίῳ χάρισμα τῆς υἱοθεσίας εἰς φανέρωσιν ἄγει

---

[135]καύσωνα CCSG

He called[200] the faithful ones the "beginners," the virtuous ones the "advanced," and the enlightened ones the "perfect"—that is to say, slaves, hired servants,[201] and sons, "the three ranks of those who are being saved."[202] For slaves are those who, because of the [1060] fear of threats, are faithful and fulfill the commandments of their master and dutifully execute that which has been entrusted to them. The hired servants are those who, because of the desire for promised blessings, "bear" with endurance "the burden of the day and the scorching heat"[203] (that is, the tribulation that is inherent in and bound to the present life because of our ancestral sentence, [1065] and the trials we experience in life as we pursue virtue). The hired servants are those who, wisely and according to their own free will, exchange the present life for the life that is to come. And sons are those who—neither because of the fear of threats nor because of the desire for promised blessings but because of the character and habit of the inclination and disposition of the soul for the good according [1070] to free will—are never separated from God, as that son to whom it has been said: "Son, you are always with me, and all that is mine is [CCSG 66] yours."[204] They are sons according to their position in grace because, in as far as it is possible, they are what God is and is believed to be according to his nature and cause. [1075]

Therefore, let us not be absent from the holy Church of God because she contains such great mysteries of our salvation according to the holy regulation of the divine symbols performed there. Through these mysteries, the Church fashions each one into the image of Christ[205]—each one of us who conducts himself properly to the very best of his ability[206]—and she reveals the gift of [1080]

---

[200]ἐκάλει; the verb is in the imperfect; "he used to call." We presume that the subject is "the blessed elder."

[201]μίσθιος; the connotation is "wage-earner."

[202]Gregory of Nazianzus, *Oration* 40.13.

[203]Mt 20.12.

[204]Lk 15.31.

[205]κατὰ Χριστόν; lit. "according to Christ."

[206]καλῶς μάλιστα πολιτευόμενον ἀναλόγως ἑαυτῳ; this phrase is translated

κατὰ Χριστὸν πολιτευόμενον[136] ἀλλὰ πάσῃ δυνάμει τε καὶ
σπουδῇ παραστήσωμεν ἑαυτοὺς ἀξίους τῶν θείων χαρισμάτων
δι᾽ ἔργων ἀγαθῶν εὐαρεστοῦντας τῷ Θεῷ μὴ ἀναστρεφόμενοι
κατὰ τὰ ἔθνη τὰ μὴ εἰδότα Θεὸν ἐν πάθει ἐπιθυμίας, ἀλλά,
καθώς φησιν ὁ ἅγιος Ἀπόστολος, νεκρώσαντες τὰ μέλη τὰ ἐπὶ
τῆς γῆς, πορνείαν, ἀκαθαρσίαν, πάθος, ἐπιθυμίαν κακήν, καὶ τὴν
πλεονεξίαν, ἥτις ἐστὶν εἰδωλολατρεία, δι᾽ ἃ ἔρχεται ἡ ὀργὴ[137]
ἐπὶ τοὺς υἱοὺς τῆς ἀπειθείας, ὀργήν τε <712c> πᾶσαν καὶ θυμὸν
καὶ αἰσχρολογίαν καὶ ψεῦδος, καί συντόμως εἰπεῖν, πάντα τὸν
παλαιὸν ἄνθρωπον, τὸν φθειρόμενον κατὰ τὰς ἐπιθυμίας τῆς
ἀπάτης, ἀποθέμενοι σὺν ταῖς πράξεσιν αὐτοῦ καὶ ταῖς ἐπιθυμίαις,
ἀξίως τοῦ Θεοῦ περιπατήσωμεν, τοῦ καλέσαντος ἡμᾶς εἰς τὴν
αὐτοῦ βασιλείαν καὶ δόξαν· ἐνδυσάμενοι σπλάγχνα οἰκτιρμοῦ,
χρηστότητα, ταπεινοφροσύνην, πραΰτητα,[138] μακροθυμίαν·
ἀνεχόμενοι ἀλλήλων ἐν ἀγάπῃ, καὶ χαριζόμενοι ἑαυτοῖς ἐάν τις
πρός τινα ἔχῃ μομφήν, καθὼς καὶ ὁ Κύριος ἐχαρίσατο ἡμῖν, ἐπὶ
πᾶσί τε τὸν σύνδεσμον τελειότητος, τὴν ἀγάπην καὶ τὴν εἰρήνην,
εἰς ἣν καὶ ἐκλήθημεν ἐν ἑνὶ σώματ, καί, ἵνα συνελὼν εἴπω, τὸν νέον
ἄνθρωπον, <712d> τὸν ἀνακαινούμενον εἰς ἐπίγνωσιν κατ᾽ εἰκόνα
τοῦ κτίσαντος αὐτόν.

Οὕτω γὰρ ἂν βιοῦντες δυνηθείημεν πρὸς τὸ τέλος ἐλθεῖν
τῶν θείων ἐπαγγελιῶν μετ᾽ ἐλπίδος ἀγαθῆς, πληρωθῆναί τε τὴν
ἐπίγνωσιν τοῦ θελήματος αὐτοῦ καὶ πάσῃ σοφίᾳ καὶ συνέσει
πνευματικῇ καρποφοροῦντες καὶ αὐξανόμενοι τῇ ἐπιγνώσει
Κυρίου, ἐν πάσῃ δυνάμει δυναμούμενοι κατὰ τὸ κράτος τῆς
δόξης αὐτοῦ, εἰς πᾶσαν οἰκοδομὴν καὶ μακροθυμίαν μετὰ χαρᾶς,

---

[136]τελειούμενον CCSG
[137]ὀργὴ τοῦ Θεοῦ CCSG
[138]πραότητα CCSG

adoption that is given through holy baptism in the Holy Spirit and that perfects each one into the image of Christ.[207] But, by all ability and diligence, "let us present"[208] ourselves worthy of the divine gifts, "pleasing God" through good works, not conducting ourselves "in the passion of lust like the Gentiles who do not know God,"[209] [1085] but as the holy apostle says: "Put to death what is earthly in you: fornication, impurity, passion, evil desire, and covetousness, which is idolatry. On account of these the wrath of God is coming on the sons of disobedience."[210] And "put away"[211] all "anger, wrath, filthy [1090] language," lies and—to speak concisely—all "the old nature which is corrupt through deceitful lusts"[212] "with its practices"[213] and lusts. But, "let us walk in a manner worthy of God, who called us into [CCSG 67] his own kingdom and glory,"[214] and "put on compassion, kindness, [1095] humility, gentleness, patience—forbearing one another" in love "and, if one has a complaint against another, forgiving each other, even as Christ has forgiven you"—and, "above all, the bond of perfection, love and peace, to which we were also called in one body."[215] [1100] If I may speak concisely: "Put on the new" nature, "which is being renewed in knowledge after the image of its creator."[216] For, when we live in this way, we may be able to come to the end of the divine promises with good hope and "to be filled with the knowledge of his will in all spiritual wisdom and understanding, bearing fruit and [1105] increasing in the knowledge of the Lord, being strengthened with all power, according to his glorious might, for all" edification "and

---

literally "who conducts himself as a citizen especially well proportionately to his own [ability]."

[207] Again, lit. "according to Christ."
[208] Cf. Rom 12.1.
[209] 1 Thess 4.5.
[210] Col 3.5–6.
[211] Col 3.8.
[212] Eph 4.22.
[213] Col 3.9.
[214] 1 Thess 2.12.
[215] Col 3.12–15.
[216] Col 3.10.

εὐχαριστοῦντες τῷ Πατρί, τῷ ἱκανώσαντι ἡμᾶς εἰς τὴν μερίδα τοῦ κλήρου τῶν ἁγίων ἐν τῷ φωτί.

<713a> Σαφὴς δὲ τῆς χάριτος ταύτης ἐστὶν ἀπόδειξις ἡ πρὸς τὸ συγγενὲς δι᾽ εὐνοίας ἑκούσιος συνδιάθεσις, ἧς ἔργον ἐστίν, ὡς Θεόν, οἰκειοῦσθαι κατὰ δύναμιν τὸν καθ᾽ ὁτιοῦν τῆς ἡμῶν ἐπικουρίας δεόμενον ἄνθρωπον, καὶ μὴ ἐᾶν ἀτημέλητον καὶ ἀπρονόητον, ἀλλὰ σπουδῇ τῇ πρεπούσῃ κατ᾽ ἐνέργειαν ἐνδείκνυσθαι ζῶσαν τὴν ἐν ἡμῖν πρός τε τὸν Θεὸν καὶ τὸν πλησίον διάθεσιν. Ἔργον γὰρ ἀπόδειξις διαθέσεως. οὐδὲν γὰρ οὔτε πρὸς δικαιοσύνην οὕτω ῥάδιόν ἐστιν, οὔτε πρὸς θέωσιν (ἵν᾽ οὕτως εἴπω) τὴν[139] πρὸς Θεὸν ἐγγύτητα καθέστηκεν ἐπιτήδειον, ὡς ἔλεος ἐκ ψυχῆς εἰς τοὺς δεομένους μεθ᾽ ἡδονῆς καὶ χαρᾶς προσφερόμενος. εἰ γὰρ Θεὸν ὁ Λόγος τὸν εὖ παθεῖν δεόμενον ἔδειξεν· Ἐφ᾽ ὅσον γὰρ ἐποιήσατε, φησίν, ἑνὶ τούτων τῶν ἐλαχίστων,[140] ἐμοὶ ἐποιήσατε. <713b> Θεὸς δὲ ὁ εἰπών, πολλῷ μᾶλλον τὸν εὖ ποιεῖν δυνάμενον καὶ ποιοῦντα, δείξει[141] ἀληθῶς κατὰ χάριν καὶ μέθεξιν ὄντα Θεόν, ὡς τὴν αὐτοῦ τῆς εὐεργεσίας εὐμιμήτως ἀνειλημμένον ἐνέργειάν τε καὶ ἰδιότητα. καὶ εἰ Θεὸς ὁ πτωχός, διὰ τὴν τοῦ δι᾽ ἡμᾶς πτωχεύσαντος Θεοῦ συγκατάβασιν, καὶ εἰς ἑαυτὸν ἑκάστου συμπαθῶς ἀναδεχομένου πάθη καὶ μέχρι τῆς συντελείας τοῦ αἰῶνος κατὰ τὴν ἀναλογίαν τοῦ ἐν ἑκάστῳ πάθους ἀεὶ δι᾽ ἀγαθότητα πάσχοντος μυστικῶς, πλέον δηλονότι κατὰ τὸν εἰκότα λόγον ἔσται Θεός, ὁ κατὰ μίμησιν τοῦ Θεοῦ διὰ φιλανθρωπίαν τὰ τῶν παθόντων πάθη δι᾽ ἑαυτοῦ θεοπρεπῶς ἐξιώμενος, καὶ τὴν αὐτὴν τῷ Θεῷ κατὰ ἀναλογίαν τῆς σωστικῆς προνοίας κατὰ διάθεσιν ἔχων δεικνύμενος δύναμιν. <713c> τίς οὖν ἄρα πρὸς ἀρετὴν οὕτω βραδύς ἐστι καὶ δυσκίνητος,

---

[139]καὶ τὴν CCSG
[140]ἐλαχίστων ἐποιήσατε CCSG
[141]δείξειεν CCSG

patience with joy, giving thanks to the Father, who has qualified us to share in the inheritance of the saints in light."[217]

And the voluntary disposition of goodwill toward our relations [1110] is the clear proof of this grace. And the work of this disposition is that the man who requires our aid becomes as much our relation as God, in as far as this is possible, and we do not leave him unnoticed [CCSG 68] and uncared for but with proper diligence we show by our action the [1115] disposition that lives in us toward God and neighbor. "For work is the proof of disposition." For he ordained[218] that nothing be more conducive for righteousness and theosis—if I may speak thus—and suitable for closeness to God than mercy from the soul administered to those in need with pleasure and joy. For, if the Word shows that [1120] the one who requires aid is God—for he says, "As you did it to one of the least of these, you did it to me"[219] and, of course, God is the one who is speaking—how much more does he show that the one who is able to do good and does it truly is God according to grace and participation, because he has assumed by successful imitation the outworking and particularity of God's own doing of good? And [1125] if the poor man is God—on account of the condescension of God, "who became poor for our sake"[220] who compassionately takes upon himself the sufferings of each one, and who, because of his goodness, always suffers mystically in proportion to the suffering in each one, "even until the end of the age"[221]—by the same principle, how much [1130] more then will he be God who, in imitation of God's love toward humanity, cures the sufferings of those who suffer through his own sufferings in a manner worthy of God and who possesses according to the proportion of God's salvific providence and displays according to his disposition the same power as God?[222] Who therefore is [CCSG 69]

[217]Col 1.9–12.
[218]We assume that Maximus is continuing to speak of the blessed elder.
[219]Mt 25.40.
[220]2 Cor 8.9.
[221]Mt 28.20.
[222]This marvelously intricate sentence in Greek does not lend itself to translation into English sentences of conventional length. We have allowed Maximus' sentence to

ὥστε μὴ ἐφίεσθαι θεότητος, οὕτως εὐώνου τε καὶ εὐπορίστου καὶ ῥᾳδίας οὔσης τῆς κτήσεως;

Ἀσφαλὴς δὲ τούτων ἐστὶ καὶ ἄσυλος φυλακή, καὶ εὐμαρὴς πρὸς σωτηρίαν ὁδός· ἧς, οἶμαι, χωρὶς κατ' ἀλήθειαν οὐδὲν ἔσται τῶν ἀγαθῶν ἀβλαβῶς τῷ ἔχοντι συντηρούμενον· ἡ αὐτοπραγία, εἴτουν ἰδιοπραγία, δι' ἧς τὰ καθ' ἑαυτοὺς σκοπεῖν τε καὶ διασκέπτεσθαι μόνους μανθάνοντες τοῦ παρ' ἄλλων διακενῆς βλάβην ἔχειν ἐλευθερούμεθα. εἰ γὰρ ἑαυτοὺς μόνους ὁρᾶν τε καὶ ἐτάζειν μάθοιμεν, οὐδέποτε τοῖς τῶν ἄλλων, ὡς δ' ἂν ἔχοντα τύχωσιν, ἐπιθησόμεθα· γινώσκοντες ἕνα μόνον κριτὴν σοφόν τε καὶ δίκαιον τὸν Θεόν, τὸν σοφῶς τε καὶ δικαίως πάντα τὰ γινόμενα κρίνοντα, καθ' ὃν γεγένηται <713d> λόγον, ἀλλ' οὐ καθ' ὃν πεφανέρωται τρόπον· ὃν ἴσως ἂν δύναιντο καὶ ἄνθρωποι κρίνειν, ἀμυδρῶς εἰς τὸ φαινόμενον βλέποντες, περὶ ὃ οὐ πάντως ἐστὶν ἡ ἀλήθεια, οὐδὲ τῶν γινομένων λόγος. Ὁ δὲ Θεὸς τὸ ἀφανές τε κίνημα τῆς ψυχῆς, καὶ τὴν ἀόρατον ὁρμήν, καὶ τὸν λόγον αὐτόν, καθ' ὃν ὥρμηται ἡ ψυχή, καὶ τὸν τοῦ λόγου σκοπόν, τουτέστι τὸ παντὸς πράγματος προεπινοούμενον τέλος βλέπων, κρίνει δικαίως, <716a> ὡς ἔφην, πάντα τὰ παρὰ τῶν ἀνθρώπων πραττόμενα ὅπερ εἰ κατορθῶσαι σπουδάσομεν, καὶ ἑαυτοῖς ἑαυτοὺς περιορίσομεν τοῖς ἐκτὸς οὐκ ἐπιφυόμενοι, οὔτε ὁρᾶν, οὔτε ἀκούειν, οὔτε λαλεῖν, τὸν ὀφθαλμόν, ἢ τὸ οὖς, ἢ τὴν γλῶσσαν τὰ τῶν ἄλλων ἀφήσομεν, εἰ μὲν οἷόν τέ ἐστι, παντελῶς, εἰ δὲ μήγε, συμπαθῶς μᾶλλον, ἀλλ' οὐ[142] μὴ ἐμπαθῶς τούτοις ἐνεργεῖν, καὶ εἰς κέρδος ἡμέτερον ὁρᾶν τε καὶ ἀκούειν, καὶ λαλεῖν ἐπιτρέποντες καὶ τοσοῦτον μόνον, ὅσον τῷ ἡνιοχοῦντι ταῦτα θείῳ λόγῳ δοκεῖ. οὐδὲν γὰρ τούτων τῶν ὀργάνων πρὸς

---

[142]ἀλλὰ CCSG

so dull and obstinate toward virtue that he does not long for deity, [1135]
since its possession is so cheap, ordinary, and easy?

A certain and safe protection for these blessings, and an easy
road to salvation—apart from which, I suppose, truly none of these
blessings will be preserved securely for the one who possesses
them—is attention to one's own actions or attention to one's private [1140]
actions,[223] whereby we are set free from purposeless injury caused by
others when we learn to look after and examine our affairs alone. For,
if we learn to consider and test ourselves alone, we will not interfere
in the affairs of others, whatever they may be, because we know that
God is the one and only wise and just judge. He wisely and justly [1145]
judges all things that come into being; he judges them according to
the principle by which they have come into being and not according
to the mode by which they have appeared. For, probably even men
are able to judge the mode, although they see dimly into that which
appears. But the truth is not to be found in all ways in that which
appears, nor is the principle of the things that are coming into being.
But God, who sees the unseen movement[224] of the soul, her invis- [1150]
ible impulse, the very principle by which the soul is set in motion,
and the aim of the principle—that is, the preconceived end of each [CCSG 70]
deed—justly judges all things done by men, as I said above. And so,
if we are diligent to mind our business and limit ourselves to our own [1155]
affairs, not becoming involved in outside matters, we will let neither
our eye see, nor our ear hear, nor our tongue speak about the affairs
of others, if indeed such is completely the case. If it is not, let us act
out of compassion and not out of passion, permitting ourselves to
see, hear, and speak only when it is beneficial for us and only to the [1160]
extent that is determined by the divine reason that animates[225] us.

pass into English unbroken in order to do our best to communicate the philosophical
exactitude with which Maximus approaches the subject of theosis.

[223]Maximus uses technical terms: αὐτοπραγία ("one's own actions") and
ἰδιοπραγία ("one's private actions").

[224]κίνημα; the word can also mean "excitement" or "emotions."

[225]ἡνιοχέω; the word means to "hold the reigns," and the term ἡνίοχος is a
"charioteer." The image therefore is that divine reason should animate our organs as
a charioteer controls a chariot.

ἁμαρτίαν ἐστὶν εὐολισθότερον, μὴ λόγῳ παιδαγωγουμένων· καὶ
οὐδὲν πάλιν πρὸς σωτηρίαν αὐτῶν ἑτοιμότερον, τάσσοντος αὐτὰ
τοῦ λόγου καὶ ῥυθμίζοντος καὶ ἐφ᾽ ἃ δεῖ καὶ βούλεται ἄγοντος.

<716b> Μὴ τοίνυν ἀμελήσωμεν κατὰ δύναμιν τοῦ πείθεσθαι
τῷ Θεῷ, καλοῦντι ἡμᾶς εἰς ζωὴν αἰώνιον καὶ μακάριον τέλος διὰ
τῆς ἐργασίας[143] τῶν αὐτοῦ θείων τε καὶ σωτηρίων ἐντολῶν, ἵνα
λάβωμεν ἔλεος, καὶ χάριν εὕρωμεν εἰς εὔκαιρον βοήθειαν· ἡ γὰρ
χάρις, φησὶν ὁ θεῖος Ἀπόστολος, μετὰ πάντων τῶν ἀγαπώντων
τὸν Κύριον ἡμῶν Ἰησοῦν Χριστὸν ἐν ἀφθαρσίᾳ, τουτέστι τῶν μετὰ
τῆς κατ᾽ ἀρετὴν ἀφθαρσίας καὶ τῆς κατὰ τὸν βίον καθαρᾶς τε καὶ
ἀνυποκρίτου σεμνότητος ἀγαπώντων τὸν Κύριον[144] ἐν τῷ ποιεῖν
αὐτοῦ τὰ θελήματα καὶ μὴ παραφθειρόντων τι τῶν θείων αὐτοῦ
προσταγμάτων.

Ταῦτα μὲν ἐγὼ περὶ τούτων διὰ τὸν τῆς ὑπακοῆς μισθόν,
κατὰ δύναμιν, ὡς ἐδιδάχθην, ἐξεθέμην, τῶν μυστικωτέρων τε
καὶ ὑψηλοτέρων ἅψασθαι μὴ τολμήσας· <716c> ἅπερ εἰ ποθεῖ τις
γνῶναι τῶν φιλομαθῶν, τοῖς περὶ τούτων τῷ ἁγίῳ Διονυσίῳ
τῷ Ἀρεοπαγίτῃ ἐνθέως πονηθεῖσιν ἐντύχοι[145] καὶ εὑρήσει κατ᾽
ἀλήθειαν μυστηρίων ἀρρήτων ἀποκάλυψιν, διὰ τῆς θείας αὐτοῦ
καὶ διανοίας καὶ γλώττης χαρισθεῖσαν τῷ τῶν ἀνθρώπων γένει,
διὰ τοὺς μέλλοντας κληρονομεῖν σωτηρίαν. καὶ εἰ μὲν πολὺ
τῆς ὑμῶν ἐπιθυμίας οὐκ ἀποπέπτωκε, τῷ Χριστῷ χάρις τῷ
χορηγῷ τῶν καλῶν, καὶ ὑμῖν τοῖς λεχθῆναι ταῦτα βιασαμένοις.
εἰ δὲ μακράν που καὶ πολὺ τῆς ἐλπίδος ἀπολείπεται, τί πάθω
ἢ τί δράσω, περὶ τὸ λέγειν ἀσθενήσας; πυγνωστὸν γάρ, οὐ[146]
τιμωρητόν, ἡ ἀσθένεια· καὶ ἀποδεκτὸν μᾶλλον, ἀλλ᾽ οὐ μεμπτὸν

[143]ἐνεργίας CCSG
[144]κύριον, ἢ σαφέστερον εἰπεῖν, τῶν ἀγαπώντων τὸν κύριον CCSG
[145]ἐτύχῃ CCSG
[146]ἀλλ᾽ οὐ CCSG

For nothing slips more easily toward sin than these organs, when they are not trained by reason; but again, nothing is more ready for salvation than they, when reason orders and arranges them and leads them to that which is necessary and what it wills. [1165]

Therefore, to the best of our ability, let us not neglect to trust in God, the one who calls us to eternal life and a blessed end through the outworking of his divine and saving commandments, "that we may receive mercy and find grace to help in time of need."[226] For, the divine apostle says, "Grace be with all who love our Lord Jesus Christ with incorruptible love,"[227] that is, those who love the Lord in the incorruptibility that comes with virtue and in the pure, sincere reverence of their lifestyle, or—to speak more clearly—those who love the Lord by doing his will and by not corrupting any of his divine ordinances. [1175]

[1170]
[CCSG 7]

Conclusion:

I have expounded the above themes to the best of my ability as I learned them, as a reward for obedience, not daring to touch the more mystical and higher things. If anyone who loves learning desires to know such things, he should consult the works of the holy Dionysius the Areopagite on these themes, works produced by great effort and inspiration. He will truly find that a revelation of ineffable mysteries has been given to the human race through his divine understanding and tongue, "for the sake of those who are to inherit salvation."[228] And, if what I have written has not fallen far below your expectations, thanks be to Christ, the one who bestows every beautiful thing, and to you who constrained me to write these things. But, if it has fallen very far below "what you had hoped,"[229] "why should I suffer," or what should I do, since I am such a weak speaker? But, "weakness should be pardoned"[230] and "not punished," and my best [1180]

[1185]

[226]Heb 4.16.
[227]Eph 6.24.
[228]Heb 1.14.
[229]Gregory of Nazianzus, *Oration* 43.82.
[230]Pseudo-Dyionysius, *On the Divine Names* 4.35.

τὸ ἐγχωροῦν καὶ ἐνδεχόμενον, καὶ μάλισθ᾿ ὑμῖν, τοῖς ἀγαπᾶν διὰ
τὸν Θεὸν προθεμένοις. καὶ Θεῷ δὲ φίλον <716d> τὸ κατὰ δύναμιν
ἄπαν γνησίως ἐκ ψυχῆς προσαγόμενον, κἂν μικρὸν συγκρίσει
μεγάλων ὑπάρχον φανήσεται· ὃς οὐδὲ τὴν χήραν τὰ δύο λεπτὰ
προσκομίσασαν ἀπώσατο, ἥτις ποτὲ ἦν ἡ χήρα αὕτη καὶ τὰ δύο[147]
λεπτά, εἴτε ψυχὴ κακίας χηρεύουσα, καὶ ὥσπερ ἄνδρα τὸν παλαιὸν
μὲν ἀποβαλομένη νόμον, οὔπω δὲ τῆς πρὸς τὸν Λόγον καὶ Θεὸν
ἄκρας συναφείας ἀξία, προσάγουσα δὲ ὅμως αὐτῷ ἀρραβῶνος
<717a> λόγῳ ὥσπερ λεπτά, τὸν τέως σύμμετρον λόγον καὶ βίον,
ἢ πίστιν καὶ ἀγαθὴν συνείδησιν, ἢ τὴν περὶ τῶν καλῶν[148] ἕξιν
καὶ ἐνέργειαν, ἢ τὴν τούτοις πρόσφορον θεωρίαν καὶ πρᾶξιν, ἢ
τὴν ἀνάλογον γνῶσιν καὶ ἀρετήν· ἢ τοὺς μικρὸν ὑπὲρ ταῦτα,
φημὶ δὲ[149] τοὺς ἐν τῷ φυσικῷ καὶ τῷ γραπτῷ νόμῳ λόγους, οὓς
ἡ ψυχὴ κεκτημένη, κατ᾿ ἔκστασιν τούτων καὶ ἄφεσιν ὡς ὅλου
βίου καὶ ζωῆς μόνῳ συναφθῆναι τῷ Λόγῳ καὶ Θεῷ βουλομένη
προσάγει, καὶ τῶν κατὰ φύσιν καὶ νόμον βιαίων τρόπων τε καὶ
θεσμῶν καὶ ἐθῶν, ὥσπερ ἀνδρῶν χηρεύειν δέχεται, εἴτε τι ἄλλο
τούτων πνευματικώτερον, καὶ μόνοις θεωρητὸν τοῖς καθαροῖς τὴν
διάνοιαν, διὰ τοῦ καθ᾿ ἱστορίαν πληρωθέντος γράμματος ὁ λόγος
αἰνίττεται. πάντα γὰρ τῷ κατὰ θεολογίαν ἐποπτικῷ συγκρινόμενα
<717b> λόγῳ, τὰ ἐν ἀνθρώποις δοκοῦντα κατ᾿ ἀρετὴν εἶναι μεγάλα,
μικρὰ τυγχάνει. πλήν γε ὅτι κἂν μικρά, καὶ ἐξ ὕλης εὐτελοῦς καὶ
οὐ πολὺ τιμίας, ἀλλ᾿ οὖν τοῖς ἐκ χρυσοῦ νομίσμασι τῆς ἐν ὕλαις
τιμιωτέρας, ἃ προσφέρουσιν οἱ εὐπορώτεροι, κατὰ τὸ ἴσον τὸν
βασιλικὸν χαρακτῆρα φέροντα, κατὰ καὶ τὸ[150] πλέον ἴσως ἔχοντα
τῆς προσαγούσης τὴν ἐξ ὅλης διαθέσεως πρόθεσιν.

Ταύτην κἀγὼ μιμούμενος τὴν χήραν, Θεῷ τε καὶ ὑμῖν,
ἠγαπημένοι, τὰ μικρὰ ταῦτα καὶ εὐτελῆ καὶ ἐξ εὐτελοῦς καὶ

---

[147]δύο ταυτῆς CCSG
[148]τὸ καλὸν CCSG
[149]δὴ CCSG
[150]om. CCSG

attempt should be accepted rather than censured, most of all by you [CCSG 72 who have dedicated yourselves to love others on account of God. [1190] Anything that is offered sincerely from the soul "to the best of one's ability is pleasing to God,"[231] even if it appears small in comparison with great things. God did not reject the widow who brought a gift [1195] of two small copper coins[232]—whoever this widow may be and her two small copper coins—perhaps the soul that is a widow to evil and has lost her husband, the old law, but is not yet worthy of the highest union with God the Word. Nevertheless, for the moment, like small copper coins, she offers speech and conduct commensurate with the principle of a first installment—that is, "faith and a good conscience,"[233] or the habit and activity in the beautiful, or the appropri- [1200] ate contemplation and practice in these things, or the proportionate knowledge and virtue, or that which is a little above these things (I am speaking about the principles in the natural and written law). And when the soul acquires these principles by stepping away and abandoning these things as the whole manner of living and life, she offers them to God, because she desires to be united with the only [1205] Word and God. She welcomes becoming a widow to the husbands of imposed practices, rules, and customs according to nature and law. Or, perhaps, through the literal sense of the text, the passage [CCSG 73] intimates something more spiritual than these interpretations, something that can be contemplated only by the pure. For, even that [1210] which seems to be great among men according to virtue is small, when compared to the highest word of contemplation according to theology. But, although they are small and made of insignificant material and not greatly valued, still they are equal to the coins of gold and precious metal that the wealthy offer, for they bear equally [1215] the royal image, and they perhaps represent greater sacrifice on the part of the widow who offers them. And, imitating this widow, I have offered to God and to you, beloved, as you requested, these small

[231]Gregory of Nazianzus, *Oration* 43.82.
[232]Cf. Mk 12.41–44, Lk 21.1–4.
[233]1 Tim 1.19.

πτωχῆς διανοίας καὶ γλώσσης προενηνεγμένα νοήματά τε καὶ ῥήματα ὥσπερ λεπτά, <717c> περὶ ὧν ἐκελεύσατε, προσενήνοχα, παρακαλῶν τὴν εὐλογημένην ὑμῶν καὶ ἁγίαν ψυχήν· πρῶτον μέν, μηδενὸς ἔτι τῶν παρ᾽ ἐμοῦ λεγομένων ἔγγραφον ζητῆσαι σημείωσιν, δυοῖν ἕνεκεν· ἑνὸς μέν, ὅτι μηδέπω τὸν φόβον ἐκτησάμην τοῦ Θεοῦ τὸν ἁγνὸν καὶ διαμένοντα, οὐδ᾽ ἀρετῆς ἕξιν στερέμνιον καὶ δικαιοσύνης ἀληθοῦς πῆξιν σταθερὰν καὶ ἀσάλευτον, τὰ μαρτυροῦντα μάλιστα τοῖς λόγοις τὸ βέβαιον· ἑτέρου δέ, ὅτι πολλῷ κλύδωνι παθῶν ἔτι δίκην θαλάσσης ἀγρίας περιδονούμενος καὶ πολὺ τοῦ θείου[151] ἀπαθείας ἀπέχων λιμένος, καὶ ἄδηλον ἔχων τοῦ βίου τὸ πέρας, οὐ βούλομαι πρὸς τοῖς ἔργοις καὶ τὸν ἐν γράμμασι λόγον ἔχειν κατήγορον. ἔπειτα δὲ τῆς εὐπειθείας χάριν, εἰ δέον ἐστίν, ἀποδεξάμενοι,[152] Χριστῷ με δι᾽ εὐχῶν παράθεσθε[153] τῷ μεγάλῳ καὶ μόνῳ <717d> Θεῷ καὶ Σωτῆρι τῶν ἡμετέρων ψυχῶν, ᾧ ἡ δόξα καὶ τὸ κράτος, σὺν τῷ Πατρὶ καὶ τῷ ἁγίῳ Πνεύματι, εἰς τοὺς αἰῶνας, ἀμήν.

---

[151]θείου τῆς CCSG
[152]ἀποδεξαμένην CCSG
[153]παραθέσθαι CCSG

and insignificant thoughts and words brought from my insignificant and poor understanding and tongue as small copper coins. I exhort [1220] your blessed and holy soul, first of all, not to seek any further written comments from me about anything that I have said, for two reasons: one is that I have not yet acquired the "pure"[234] and "enduring fear" of God, the firm habit of virtue, and the calm and unshaken stability [1225] of true righteousness, which above all witness to the reliability of words. But, the other reason is that, since I am still driven about by a great storm of passions like a raging sea, and since I am far away [CCSG 74] from the harbor of divine impassibility and have an uncertain limit to my life, I do not wish to have my written speech as an accuser in [1230] addition to my deeds. Nevertheless, if it is right, after you receive the gift of my ready obedience, commend me through your prayers to Christ, the great and only God and Savior of our souls, "to whom be glory and dominion" with the Father and the Holy Spirit "forever, amen."[235]

[234]Cf. Ps 19.9.
[235]Rev 1.6.

Bibliography of English Translations of the Works of Maximus the Confessor

Ambigua to Thomas and Second Letter to Thomas. Trans. Joshua Lollar. Corpus Christianorum in Translation. Turnhout: Brepols, 2009.

The Church, the Liturgy and the Soul of Man: The "Mystagogia" of St. Maximus the Confessor. Trans. Julian Stead. Still River, MA: St. Bede's Publications, 1982.

The Cosmic Mystery of Jesus Christ. Trans. Paul M. Blowers and Robert Louis Wilken. Popular Patristics Series 25. Crestwood, NY: St. Vladimir's Seminary Press, 2003.

On Difficulties in the Church Fathers: The Ambigua *of Maximus the Confessor*. Trans. Maximos Constas. Dumbarton Oaks Medieval Library. Cambridge: Harvard University Press, 2014.

Disputation with Pyrrhus. Trans. Joseph P. Farrell. South Canaan, PA: St Tikhon's Monastery Press, 2014.

The Life of the Virgin: Maximus the Confessor. Trans. Stephen Shoemaker. New Haven: Yale University Press, 2012.

Maximus the Confessor. Trans. Andrew Louth. The Early Church Fathers. New York: Routledge, 1996.

Maximus Confessor: Selected Writings. Trans. George C. Berthold. Classics of Western Spirituality. New York: Paulist Press, 1985.

St. Maximus the Confessor's Questions and Doubts. Trans. Despina Prassas. DeKalb: Northern Illinois University Press, 2010.

Scripture Index

We hope this book has been enjoyable and edifying for your spiritual journey toward our Lord and Savior Jesus Christ.

One hundred percent of the net proceeds of all SVS Press sales directly support the mission of St Vladimir's Orthodox Theological Seminary to train priests, lay leaders, and scholars to be active apologists of the Orthodox Christian Faith. However, the proceeds only partially cover the operational costs of St Vladimir's Seminary. To meet our annual budget, we rely on the generosity of donors who are passionate about providing theological education and spiritual formation to the next generation of ordained and lay servant leaders in the Orthodox Church.

Donations are tax-deductible and can be made at www.svots.edu/donate. We greatly appreciate your generosity.

To engage more with St Vladimir's Orthodox Theological Seminary, please visit:

www.svots.edu
online.svots.edu
www.svspress.com
www.instituteofsacredarts.com

POPULAR PATRISTICS SERIES

ST VLADIMIR'S SEMINARY PRESS
1-800-204-2665 • www.svspress.com